THE SUPER ORGANIC GARDENER

Everything You Need to Know
About a Vegan Garden

MATTHEW APPLEBY

WHITE OWL

AN IMPRINT OF PEN & SWORD BOOKS LTD.
YORKSHIRE – PHILADELPHIA

First published in Great Britain in 2018 by
PEN & SWORD WHITE OWL
An imprint of
Pen & Sword Books Ltd
Yorkshire - Philadelphia

ISBN 9781526737472

Printed and bound by Replika Press Pvt. Ltd.
Design: Paul Wilkinson.

Pen & Sword Books Limited incorporates the imprints of Atlas,
Archaeology, Aviation, Discovery, Family History, Fiction, History, Maritime, Military, Military Classics,
Politics, Select, Transport, True Crime, Air World, Frontline Publishing, Leo Cooper, Remember When,
Seaforth Publishing,
The Praetorian Press, Wharncliffe Local History, Wharncliffe Transport,
Wharncliffe True Crime and White Owl.

For a complete list of Pen & Sword titles please contact
PEN & SWORD BOOKS LIMITED
47 Church Street, Barnsley, South Yorkshire, S70 2AS, United Kingdom
E-mail: enquiries@pen-and-sword.co.uk
Website: www.pen-and-sword.co.uk

Or
PEN AND SWORD BOOKS
1950 Lawrence Rd, Havertown, PA 19083, USA
E-mail: Uspen-and-sword@casematepublishers.com
Website: www.penandswordbooks.com

CONTENTS

FOREWORD

by Cleve West, Chelsea Flower Show best in show winner and vegan organic gardener

ACKNOWLEDGEMENTS

Cleve West for his foreword; Kath Gavin of Hulme Community Garden Centre; David Graham of the Vegan Organic Network, Garden Organic, Veganuary, West 6 Garden Centre, Hortus Loci. Jon Wright, Janet Brookes of Pen & Sword; my editor, Carol Trow; Rachel Webb, Bethan Norris and Janet Watson for all their help and last, but by no means least, William and Ted, my children.

Unless otherwise specified, all images are the copyright of the author.

It's around 10 years since I visited Iain Tolhurst's Hardwick Estate in Oxfordshire to learn about his organic, stock-free system that excludes fertiliser derived from animals. I was vegetarian at the time and hadn't quite made the connection with vegan ethics but was already experimenting with green manure and had, from the outset, adopted a 'live-and-let-live' policy at our West London allotment, where nothing was killed deliberately. In essence, this is what veganism is about, a way of life that seeks to avoid, where practically possible, all forms of exploitation and cruelty to animals for food, clothing and any other purpose. Of course, there are always going to be unavoidable, accidental deaths among smaller, unseen creatures. The aim is to avoid the deliberate, unnecessary ones.

After becoming a fully-fledged ethical vegan in 2015, I started to do a little research of my own and found that not only are animal products the leading cause of the most common diseases in the western world, but also that the negative impact of animal agriculture on climate change and the wider environment (rainforest destruction, species extinction, pollution and ocean depletion to name a few) is reason enough to adopt a plant-based diet.

The facts are staggering and, in truth, disturbing. But challenging the morality of people's eating habits that have been endorsed for centuries by culture, tradition, convenience and the propaganda from the food and pharmaceutical industries isn't easy. People don't like being told what to do at the best of times let alone when it goes against everything they've been taught since birth. However, thanks to the internet, (which has helped expose the truth behind animal agriculture) veganism is at last being taken seriously and, with over 1 per cent of the UK now adopting a plant-based diet, being vegan shows genuine concern for environmental issues and the unnecessary commodification of animals on an unimaginable scale.

So, I was delighted when Matthew asked me to write this

Cleve West.

foreword for this book. Gardeners are a sensitive bunch and, in my experience, most already consider themselves environmentalists. They are well-placed, therefore, to become a driving force to educate others about the challenges this planet faces from the increasing threat of climate change and how to feed an ever-growing population.

The vegan movement is gathering pace, particularly with the young who are concerned for the future of this wonderful planet and its inhabitants and who can see the benefits of a kinder, more compassionate world. But it's not exclusively their gig. Old farts like me are welcome too and I can honestly say that my only regret I have about becoming vegan is not having done it a whole lot sooner.

INTRODUCTION

Super-organic, clean, vegan growing means you, as an individual, are not only doing something good environmentally, but you also will feel better about yourself.

On a worldwide scale, super organic vegan food production could mean more efficient land use. This is because animal farming uses 85 per cent of agricultural land. One-third of humanity's freshwater footprint relates to animal products – up to 76 trillion gallons. And animal agriculture is responsible for an estimated 18 per cent of greenhouse gas emissions.

Organic, plant-based diets mean fewer cancers and allergies as well as a reduction in diabetes, heart and gut illness. They also avoid the transmission of E. coli, salmonella, BSE, bird flu and other animal-borne diseases to humans.

UK animal consumption is more than one billion 'units' a year. But it is the animals you don't eat that cost the most environmentally, and suffer the most. The dairy farming industry has as much involvement in animal cruelty and environmental damage as the meat industry. Thus, by opting for super organic vegan food production, you are no longer supporting practices linked to both animal-related cruelty and diseases.

To you as a gardener, all this may not seem to mean much. But gardening supports environmentally damaging animal farming in several ways – the vast use of animal by-products being just one. Fortunately, changing how you garden is straightforward. Firstly, just don't use products that you think might be harmful to the environment. Then, remove those that might have been produced through the exploitation

Forest gardening is unrealistic for most people due to a lack of space.

or death of animals. Next, replace with organic fertiliser and compost; striving to cause the least suffering to the planet and its creatures, while still gardening as successfully as possible, is the objective.

Using the permaculture method of zoning from 0-5, you can design super organic gardens, from windowsill to wilderness: in size, the average yard or garden is between a window box and a forest. This 0-5 numbering system signifies how far the plants are from your house. The further

away the area, the less attention it needs. Zone zero and one could be the home, two the yard, three might be the allotment and four an outlying field. Forest gardening in zone five is unrealistic for most gardeners because of lack of space. Neither *The Good Life*-style self-sufficiency nor proper seven-year rotational production with associated large-scale wild spaces for wildlife and beneficial insects are viable options for most people. So this book is about working on an average domestic scale.

Start with the basics; where will be best to place raised beds and a shed/greenhouse ...

Start with the basics; where will be best to place raised beds and a shed/greenhouse (if you have space)? Look at aspect. Don't dig the soil so you can retain its structure. Instead, sow cover crops/green manure seeds to suppress weeds, build productive soil and help control pests and diseases. Then, add organic matter to aid fertility. Plan the first crop in your rotation (usually potatoes) plus companion crops. Plant perennials, fruit bushes and trees; don't forget flowers – growing this way should not be joyless, and flowers help pollination. Add compost and sow/plant seasonal veg. Water and fertilise.

Then harvest and eat, making sure you include all the essential nutrients in your plant-based diet.

IN 2016, THERE were 563,000 vegans in the UK and more than two million in the USA. There has been a 500 per cent explosion in numbers of people going vegan from 2014-17, according to GlobalData. In the UK 3.25 per cent of people are vegetarian or vegan.

Organic sales in the USA totalled around $47 billion in 2016, reflecting new sales of almost $3.7 billion from the previous year. Organic food now accounts for more than 5 per cent of total food sales in the USA. The Soil Association's 2017 Organic Market Report shows the UK organic market is growing and worth £2.09 billion, around 1.5 per cent of the UK food and drink market.

Having spent 15 years writing about the horticulture trade, I know how horticultural production works and what products can help you succeed, whatever type of gardening you try. I'm probably more relaxed about this than some organic hardliners, who want a closed system with nothing bought in.

Apart from growing, this style of gardening is about treating garden wildlife properly. We only call these creatures 'wild' because we haven't shoved them in cages yet, so maybe freelife is a better term. I recommend no wildlife feeding. Feeding upsets nature's balance. Backyard fish, bees, chickens and worms in wormeries become pets for gardeners. Worms, insect pollinators and birds help plants grow. But they don't belong to you. Using this system should mean there will be plenty of animals on your plot without you needing to own them.

Wildlife and wild plants will add biodiversity to the plot. If they take away some yield, so what? Through using deterrents, rather than weed and creature killers, managing wild plants and animals together is achievable. Some management is important, or you are probably not gardening at all, just looking after a bit of nature.

If you don't want to use the stuff off the slaughterhouse floor and want to control what you use to grow in, avoiding peat and animal inputs, read on. As you read, you will find out about how to manage garden wildlife, learn which plants are straightforward to grow (and their nutritional values) and even discover new ideas about how to eat them.

SO, WHY BE A SUPER ORGANIC VEGAN GARDENER?

'Growing your own' is the ultimate way to ensure the provenance of what you eat. Fruit and veg gardening is becoming increasingly popular, as lengthy allotment waiting lists demonstrate, but I believe gardeners are often unaware that what they grow is not as clean and healthy as it could be.

When I talk to gardeners about super-organic gardening and vegan gardening, they often seem unfamiliar with the concept. Typical questions are: Isn't all gardening vegetables? What do you eat? How is it grown? What would happen to all the animals if everyone did it? Isn't eating meat natural, like the cavemen? Isn't it harder? If you cut a worm in half, what happens then? How do gardens eat meat?

I explain and people usually get the concept. More and more people do. Most vegetarians realise that taking the next step to become a vegan makes sense because dairy, leather, honey, wool, silk and egg production causes suffering to animals – and because animal farming is bad for the environment. But how many organic gardeners realise their pastime supports that type of farming?

If you are committed to non-violence in life, should you allow others to kill in order to produce your food? Anyone can grow food. Not many would want to raise and kill their own animals to eat. 250m tonnes of meat are eaten worldwide a year, growing by 5m tonnes a year. That's 40kg of meat a year each. But you don't have to. We're not cavemen.

Half of vegetarians 'go veggie' for health reasons. Half do it for the environment. A Venn diagram would show plenty do it for both reasons. Green gardeners do it for the environment and/or their health. Super green gardeners do it for the environment x2, their health x2 – and for the animals.

Call it vegan, ethical, clean, stock-free farming, super organic, organic+ or veganic gardening, this is a method of horticulture taken on for moral and health reasons. Gardening this way will ensure a minimal amount of exploitation or harm to animals and the environment. Basically, this is making the positive choice to do 'no shit' (actually

Not many would want to raise and kill their own animals to eat.

animal manure – or blood, fish and bone, or exploitation) gardening.

The big question is, if you care about what you eat, then why not care about how you grow?

The number of US households that use exclusively all-natural fertiliser, insect, and weed controls increased from an estimated five million households in 2004 to 12 million in 2008 according to results of National Gardening Association's 2004 and 2008 Environmental Lawn and Garden surveys.

These people avoid manufactured inorganic substances for garden plants, and they may understand wildlife's role in the garden more sympathetically than

conventional gardeners.

But how many join the two together when they buy or grow food? Riverford Organic Farms sells organic meat in its box veg schemes, for instance, because even if your food is pesticide-free, GM-free, wholefood, locally-grown, environmentally sound and green, how can animal farming and slaughter be cruelty free? And how can rearing animals be an effective use of farming land? This means to be properly green, you need to stop exploiting the earth. And animal farming puts too high a cost on the land compared to plant farming.

Just as being a vegetarian is a stepping stone to the logical conclusion of going vegan, then eating organic is a step towards growing veganically – without animal inputs, taking green gardening to its logical conclusion. This means rejecting animal by-products such as blood, fish, bone hoof, horn and manure. And it means growing to allow wildlife to thrive. That's it really.

THE PRICE OF ANIMAL FARMING

Piling on horse manure, or boosting crops with pelleted poultry manure, bonemeal or hoof and horn, means you are complicit in the factory farmed animal production industry. More than eight billion animals (10m pigs, 15m sheep, 16m turkeys, 975m broiler chickens, 2.6m cows, plus 2.6 billion shellfish and 4.5 billion fish) die a year in the UK. Animals are stunned by bolts before having their throats cut. The stunning doesn't always work. Gas and electric techniques are coming in. The EU Scientific Veterinary

Committee estimate that around 5-10 per cent of cattle are not stunned effectively with the captive bolt. Animal rights charity Viva! estimates that four million sheep may regain consciousness each year before they die. Before being killed, birds' heads are supposed to be immersed in an electrified water bath in an attempt to cause unconsciousness.

Halal and kosher killings may not involve stunning animals (never with kosher animal slaughtering). The RSPCA argues that killing animals without stunning them causes 'unnecessary suffering', while activist group PETA calls halal slaughter 'prolonged torment', saying the animals 'fight and gasp for their last breath, struggling to stand while the blood drains from their necks'. The British Veterinary Association calls for all animals to be stunned before slaughter, while the Farm Animal Welfare Council says cutting an animal's throat is 'such a massive injury [that it] would result in very significant pain and distress in the period before insensibility supervenes'.

If your gardening relies on slaughterhouse by-products, or the by-products of animal farming, then you support this slaughter. If your personal ethics mean you don't want to do this, then there is another way. If you have health or environmental concerns about growing using animals, then why not try the alternative? This involves making your own compost and fertilisers, letting 'pests' live, allowing wildlife to be wild (and even creating habitats for them) and avoiding exploiting any animals to further your hobby.

BACKGROUND

In my native Cumbria, foot and mouth disease wrecked farming in 2001. Some 10m sheep and cows were slaughtered and the disease cost the country £8bn. The epidemic was probably caused by pigs which had been fed infected swill that had not been properly heat-sterilised. This rubbish is believed to have contained remains of infected meat that had been illegally imported to Britain.

Cumbria also has a story to tell about land used to rear animals. My family home in Keswick flooded three times, in 2005, 2009 and 2015. It had never flooded before. When I say flooded, I mean wrecked. It took 6-8 months each time before

Sheep farming at Buttermere in the English Lake District.

My flooded home.

Periodic food scares, such as dioxin contamination in animal tissue, BSE and CJD have caused spikes in vegetarianism …

the house was habitable again. On a big scale, tourism (which is the local economy – sheep farming isn't) was ruined. Fixing it all costs many millions, including a £6m river wall built between the floods of 2009 and 2015 (that didn't work). On a smaller scale, all your stuff gets soaked. You get stressed every time it rains. And you can't move because your house is devalued.

Why did it flood? Heavy rain of course. But the Lakes are always rainy. Lakes village Seathwaite used to boast it was the rainiest place in England. Not such a proud boast now.

Environmental journalist George Monbiot talks about sheep-wrecking – the stripping of the fells of trees for pasture. The old wooded fell-sides are bare and let water flood into the valley – fast. He advocates re-wilding, which is letting the scrub and trees come back and allowing the becks to meander unfettered by man. Shepherd James Rebanks gives a compelling argument against this in his book *A Shepherd's Life* (2015), which portrays traditional sheep farming in the Lakes over the last thousand years, with little change until the last hundred.

Global warming means less slow-melting snow and more rain, which flows down all at once. Privatised water companies keep reservoirs high to keep up profits. Building on flood plains makes flooding worse, but the bigger issue is how to calm the waters high up in the fells. Forestry Commission spruce plantings are so dense they let little water in. Conversely, they are good for red squirrels – until the trees are felled. So, a new wild landscape of native plants could be the answer,

Animal manure.

rather than a stripped, micromanaged massive farm, which is centuries old, but is decreasing in production value. Defra statistics show LFA (less favoured area) grazing farm income had fallen to just £19,000 a year in 2016. There is a lot more money to be made from tourism. Compensation for animal diseases such as BSE has also been enormous. The European Commission said the total level of aid involved is more than £313m and is aimed at providing assistance to the rendering industry, the slaughtering industry, supplementary compensation on steers and heifers and a publicity campaign for meat.

Periodic food scares, such as dioxin contamination in animal tissue, BSE and CJD, have caused spikes in vegetarianism. The horsemeat scandal that broke in Western Europe during early 2013 may have had a similar impact.

I turned vegetarian in 1985, along

with thousands of others, after listening to The Smiths' album *Meat is Murder*. I went vegan after meeting a vegan girl in 1999. I've lapsed, as so many others do. But since started working in gardening in 2003, I have become interested in veganism in a more holistic way. And that means growing your own food, veganically. My allotment is 13m x 10m, I have a bit of garden, and I garden indoors on the windowsill.

The idea is to supplement diet with home grown and to guarantee at least some of what you eat is grown in the way you would want it to be. So last year I decided; no more manure. Or peat, because it's too risky for the environment to lose. In spring, I started off seeds such as broad beans in coir in pots under cover in a mini greenhouse. And yes – coir is imported and has its own travel miles issues. I planted cover crops to add some humus, nitrogen and minerals to the soil. I also started courgettes, sunflowers, tomatoes and squash off in this way.

I already had the perennial 'crowns' of rhubarb and asparagus planted for a guaranteed spring crop. Strawberry runners are the same. Lilies, tulips and daffodils came up as normal. Plantable onion 'sets' (little onions) are buyable by the gramme. Garlic cloves went in. Raspberries, blackcurrants, redcurrants, bilberries, blackberries and Jerusalem artichokes flourished, as well as a load of herbs. There is also an apple tree, plum tree, peach tree and cherry tree on the 10x13m plot.

My compost heaps needed improving because I knew that without them, I'd lack the organic matter the manure gave me. So, on every visit I make compost and fertiliser and add wood chip.

I do my anti-mindful ten things, examples of which are: bike there, hoe, prune with secateurs, water, make fertiliser by putting borage in a bucket of water, tie in floppy plants, mulch with a bit of wood chip, and chuck green stuff on the compost heap then turn it over. I also eat the neighbours' blackberries (in season), fix up benches and give the children jobs, then stop them fighting with hoes, rakes, and secateurs.

In early March, I plant potatoes after buying chitted sprouting 'early' varieties. I also use potatoes that have started sprouting in the kitchen cupboard. I also spread/plant direct rocket seed, radish seed, parsnip seed and that's about it.

Seasonally, at other times of the year, I may sow a cover crop or plant young plants or clear old plants or prepare the soil to plant or have a barbecue or sit around or have fire or barrow wood chip, or just sit around. It's a plot of verbs.

My top tips for gardening without cruelty can end up looking like a list of what not to do – no animal manure, no blood, fish or bone, no slug killer, no worm farms, no digging, no chickens and not being nasty to wild (free) life.

To put it more positively, make your own compost, make your own fertiliser, grow cover crops of green manure, leave wild areas for wildlife and beneficial insects, use crop rotation techniques and hoe your weeds.

The ideal is of a self-sufficient system based on local materials like compost, garden waste and leaves. My aim is to reverse engineer traditional gardening, not only taking on board organic methods,

Harvesting Jerusalem artichokes.

The hardline Ethical Vegan/Rights-Based view is that all animals have the right to be left alone and not killed or used as property ...

but also the ultimate ethical method, which is not to exploit animals at all when growing plants.

There's a social element too. For instance, at the allotment show where we meet to exhibit ugly/comedy vegetables and jam, (vegan) cakes and our best fruit and veg, all in the hope of winning a few rosettes. There's also a pumpkin carving event on bonfire night, and a spring plant sale. Most of these activities are transferable to the back garden, the indoor garden, and the community garden. There's the self-satisfaction of not exploiting animals, and of giving animals a habitat, and the knowledge that anything you produce is a win, and if you don't get much of a crop, then at least you had a nice time trying.

The central message is that veganic gardeners believe animal manures are harmful to the soil and potentially human health and also involve exploitation and cruelty to animals. They know that gardening with cleaner inputs is better for the whole environment. The system uses vegetable waste, mulches and no-dig methods to maintain soil fertility. All this avoids any possible connection to BSE, bird flu, CJD, salmonella and e-coli and other animal spread diseases (e.g.

A LANDMARK PAPER from Newcastle University, Nutritional Composition of Organic Crop Foods, published in the *British Journal of Nutrition* in 2015, concludes that organically grown crops contain significantly higher concentrations of nutritionally desirable antioxidants and lower levels of undesirable cadmium (a toxic heavy metal) and pesticide residues.

The results of this meta-analysis showed that organic crops were of a much higher nutritional quality than their non-organic counterparts. Thus super organic vegan produce gives potential protection against cancers, diabetes and cardiovascular and neurodegenerative diseases.

ProVeg International is a food awareness organisation with the mission to reduce global animal consumption by 50% by the year 2040. Director Jimmy Pierson says by 2057, we could have curbed climate change, and through individual action, and food emissions are down 70 per cent. Nature has re-wilded and wild animals are abundant. People are healthier mentally and physically, with heart disease down 40 per cent, type 2 diabetes gone and obesity no longer a concern. The resulting savings in healthcare-related costs are up to $100 billion.

Everyone has enough food. Soils are restored, meaning more nutritious food.How? 'We just started substituting meat with plant-based alternatives. By doing so, we put an end to arguably one of the greatest crimes of our time: the abuse and exploitation of animals'.

If you really want to put something back into the environment rather than taking from the earth, think seriously about greening your plot.

That doesn't just mean doing the basics of installing a water butt to harvest rain water from the shed roof. It means not using pesticides, peat, non-organic fertilisers, plastics or mains water if you want to be hair shirt and ascetic about your green-ness.

Positive steps to carbon neutrality can include installing a solar panel on your shed roof, if the roof doesn't already have plants covering the top (and indeed the walls). A solar panel is unlikely to be economically advantageous, but you have to weigh up the pros of being green with the cons of it not always saving you cash.

diphtheria) that may linger in what gardeners put in.

Gardening this way means you keep soil fertile by using green manures, cover crops, green wastes, veg compost and minerals. No animal manure, but there's no reason not to use nitrogen-rich human urine and composted human manure (if it's from someone who eats a vegan diet – I'm not joking!).

As veganism has become more mainstream, a kind of Vegan spectrum has emerged.

The Reducetarian position is a more relaxed one – a flexible, generally plant-based diet. The danger here is you will be argued down as being a hypocrite. The ethical gardening version of this would be to kill the odd slug, squish the occasional bug, feed the birds using bought food because you feel sorry for them in winter, use a bit of shop-bought compost (maybe with a bit of peat in) or fertiliser. This is the 'vegan celebrity on Twitter' stance – singer Robbie Williams has said he's a vegan apart from 'burger Sundays'.

The hardline Ethical Vegan/ Rights-Based view is that all animals have the right to be left alone and not killed or used as property. You would never kill anything, or buy anything, or do anything to disturb the natural balance. This is the 'hair shirt Marxist' stance.

Vegfest UK's Tim Barfoot, who now organises more than 150 vegan festivals in the UK annually, goes for a compromise view:

'A softly-softly, gentle, friendly, flexible, loving, supportive, nourishing, encouraging, fun, informative, educative approach that has an ethical veganism core

philosophy on the inside, but a flexible exterior which adapts to the environment and surroundings in terms of emphasis. If that means focusing on plant-based foods, on environmental concerns, on health issues, on sustainable food programmes or on any facet of veganism, so be it.'

Gardeners can be complacent, believing just because they grow plants that they are environmentally positive. Those plants release oxygen and eat CO2 and can be eaten so you don't have to buy them, which cuts transport emissions.

To build on this:

• Use a wheelbarrow to cart heavy items to the plot rather than driving them there, if you can.

• Hoe a lot rather than using weed killer. Plant densely and use a no-dig method to avoid bringing weed seeds to the top. Cut out chemicals and use green manure. Make compost using food and garden waste.

• Create habitats for wildlife by leaving wild patches, then leave the wildlife alone to thrive. Grow 'bee-friendly' plants like poppies, lavender and sunflowers and encourage birds with feeders and berry plants.

• Go vegan. There's no better way to save the planet. It takes at least three times the amount of water to feed a meat eater compared with that used to feed a vegan. Vegan diets can produce fewer greenhouse gas emissions than meat-based diets. There's the health and moral reasons too. ✻

HACKS/TOP TIPS

• Stock-free organics is about living with the land. It's about eating well without causing damage to plants and habitats.

• Using fertiliser from within the land is more sustainable, so brought in manures and chemical fertilisers do not optimise the value of your land. It is unethical to use someone else's land on yours. Produce your own fertility on site and don't steal it from somewhere else. Close the loop.

• Feed the ground with nitrogen from the air, then phosphate, potash and recycled organic matter.

• Use compost/leaf mould/green manure to build soil fertility. This works on a commercial and garden scale, as shown at Iain Tolhurst's stock-free farm in Oxfordshire and at numerous Vegan Organic Network member plots. It cuts food miles, brings in no pathogens, and involves healthy outdoor work and, potentially, builds community and sustainability.

• Rotate crops to avoid pests and diseases and add biodiversity for pest control so you have balanced insect life on the plot.

• Eliminate exploitation of animals and chemicals.

• Produce compost and fertiliser on site; it's ethical and sustainable. Conventional fertilisers use oil and can pollute.

• Remember, livestock uses land, water and requires importation of food such as soy to feed them, as well as causing deforestation, water pollution and soil erosion.

THE FIRST PRACTICAL STEPS

ASSESS YOUR PLOT

- Know your plot. Most plants grow best if they get both sunlight and rain.

- Which way does it face? North facing is colder and damper. South facing is warmer and lighter. East gets morning light and west gets afternoon/evening light.

- Where is the shelter? Northerly and easterly winds are cold. Westerlies are warmer but stronger.

- Where is the shade? Not much will thrive here.

- Plan where as much as what you want to plant. Rotate what you plant as certain plants will take certain nutrients up. Plant cover crops in between main crops.

- Build raised beds.

Most new allotments include raised beds. Growing veg in a raised bed can help you control the soil's moisture, fertility and weediness. It's easy to access too. On the other hand, these high-sided grow-boxes take up more space than just growing in the ground and feel more artificial because you are less connected with the earth beneath your feet. Also, on the downside, slugs like the corners under the beds' wooden sides. But, filled with soil mix, they provide the excellent drainage needed to grow vegetables and flowers.

Raised beds reduce soil compaction because you don't stand on them, help you get organised because they are more regimented than open ground growing and also warm up quicker in the spring. You can also grow plants closer together.

Ready-made slot-in raised bed products take out the need for a carpentry degree. Nevertheless, you might want to make your own, so here's how to make one:

- You will need: pressure treated softwood planks such as larch wood (25mmx150mm); stakes for every 1m (1,000mm x 50mm x 50mm); galvanised screws or nails. Keeping things simple, the basic raised bed should not test your joinery skills too much.

- Position the bed north-south for maximum sun exposure.

- Clear the site of weeds and level it.

- Mark out the beds with stakes and string, and check the levels.

- Drive in the rest of the stakes at the corners and every 1.5m to 60cm below ground to support the sides. You can check they are straight vertically and horizontally with a spirit level.

- Nail or screw the sides to the retaining stakes.

- Keep the bottom of the sides 50cm below ground. Fix the next row of boards to the stakes on top of the bottom layer.

- Break up the soil surface to improve drainage. Add hardcore if your bed is deep. Enrich the soil with manure and new topsoil.

- You can paint or stain your wooden beds. You can also seal gaps with waterproof self-

Building a raised bed on legs-avoids back pain, weed seed spread and the height prevents some animals climbing in ...

adhesive tape on the inside.
• A timber post raised bed needs a 400mm trench half filled with gravel for the timber post 'fence'. Butt your posts together in the trench, making sure they are all standing at the same height. You are best advised to pour in a 200mm layer of concrete to fix the posts and to line the sides of the bed with a waterproof membrane.

Brick and railway sleeper raised beds are also options.
Building a raised bed on legs-avoids back pain, weed seed spread and the height prevents some animals climbing in and nibbling your seedlings. Good for wheelchair gardeners too. 🌿

WINDOWSILL/ WINDOWBOX GARDENING

ZONE ZERO

In permaculture (the term defining an agri/horticulture system intended to be self-sufficient and sustainable) you zone garden areas, as discussed in the introduction. Zone zero is nearest the house.

To set up the windowsill garden you need pots, or a window box. When buying a window box, you need at least 15-20cm depth for the roots, drainage holes at the bottom, drip tray underneath and a tie to make sure the box or pot doesn't fall off.

For the window ledge, metal boxes work best with cardboard liners to insulate plant roots. Wood is good but can get wet and heavy, while plastic is easiest to use but environmentally the worst.

In this space, bought compost works best. You can't afford to have vine weevils, weed seeds or poor performing compost in such a small area. Without using compost from a hot heap you may get these things. Otherwise, loam soil gives the compost mix structure and has sand, silt and clay in fairly equal amounts. Sieve garden soil or you can make loam from sieved stacked turves rotted down under a tarpaulin for at least a year. Or buy a bag of loam.

Homemade loam ideally needs to be sterilised, using a specialist kit or by sieving and microwaving at three minutes per kilo, or cooking at 80 degrees on a tray. Add leaf mould for humus or use coir or peat-free soil conditioner. Then add an equal amount of sharp sand (a gritty builders' sand). You don't need high nutrients for seedlings. Sieve and mix. Fill the box until compost is 2.5-5cm below the lip. In a pot, you need drainage holes and crocks in the bottom to aid drainage. Plant seeds: salads, herbs, dwarf French beans, radishes, tomatoes and spring onions.

You can put the box in a large container of water until the top gets damp; you'll know the entire box has been watered. Or water from the top until it comes out of the holes at the bottom of the pot.

Indoors, you can grow small crops

On the ledge, grow seeds or beans such as: cress, alfalfa, chickpeas and mung beans ...

with a big kick such as microgreens, wheatgerm and beansprouts. Sprinkle seeds on to trays containing 25mm potting media (compost) or on to damp kitchen towel, in a seed tray or plastic box with drainage. After watering, place the seeds on a warm windowsill. Water and cut.

Then, you can cook and store these and other crops. Alternatively, eat raw to maximise nutritional value that may be lost in cooking. Raw eaters also often don't mind fermentation into sauerkraut or preserving into jam. Typical foods included in raw food diets are fruits, vegetables, nuts, seeds, and sprouted grains and legumes.

Among raw vegans there are some subgroups such as fruitarians, juicearians, or sproutarians. Fruitarians eat primarily or exclusively fruits, berries, seeds, and nuts. Juicearians process their raw plant foods into juice. Sproutarians adhere to a diet consisting mainly of sprouted seeds.

You need 6-8 hours of sun for growth so adding a supplemental UV light source in winter will help crops grow. On the ledge, grow seeds or beans such as: cress, alfalfa, chickpeas and mung beans.

Plant tops and bottoms of vegetables in pots. They will grow new leaves you can eat. Tops: carrots, swedes, turnips. Bottoms: cos lettuce, leeks, onions, salad onions. Repot potted herbs from the supermarket in new compost with liquid seaweed fertiliser added, or plant supermarket parsley outside.

Outside, on the patio, small spaces need dwarf plants, compact fruit trees, strawberries, potatoes and herbs in pots, bags and containers.

SOIL – WHY SO IMPORTANT

Many pieces of gardening advice begin with lectures on the importance of the soil. It's fundamental to successful growing. This is no different. Vegan super organic gardeners need to look after and safeguard their soil from erosion. 'Guardianship' of soil is the watchword.

This means plants, green manures or mulches grown on top to protect the earth, and a no-dig system underneath to avoid upsetting the ecosystem. This helps nutrient uptake and looks after the micro-organisms and worms that will look after your plot.

Being broad in your growing approach helps avoid crop failure. Vegan super organic gardeners need to grow a variety of crops to avoid one crop draining too much of certain nutrients from the soil, rotating where and what you plant will reduce soil depletion. Just as you might eat more fruit and veg for gut health, add more plant-based organic matter compost for soil health.

Mulches protect the soil from water loss and stop weeds growing. Use hay and leaves, which will feed the soil as they decompose. Garden waste is good too.

WHAT TO DO

Check your soil to see whether it is clay, sandy, loam or has other qualities. Clay is sticky, sandy is thin and loam is perfect. Whatever type your soil is, add organic matter to bulk the soil up and to improve nutrient content and water capacity, as well as making the soil less prone to compaction.

Clay soils are dense and heavy but have plenty of nutrients. They retain water and stay cold in winter then take a while to warm up and dry out in summer.

Sandy soils are light, warm, dry and are often acidic and low in nutrients. These soils have quick water drainage and are easy to work. They are quicker to warm up in spring than clay soils, but dry out in summer and have low nutrient levels, which are easily washed away by rain.

A loam soil is a mixture of sand, silt and clay. These soils are fertile, easy to work with and provide good drainage. They are a perfect balance of soil particles, but still benefit from topping up with additional organic matter.

A silt soil is more unusual. They are light and moisture retentive with high fertility, drain and hold moisture well.

Whatever type your soil is, add organic matter to bulk the soil up and to improve nutrient content and water capacity ...

Other soils are acidic peaty and alkaline chalky. They will need their pH balanced. The ideal pH is 6. You can test this with a shop-bought machine. Add lime to balance acid soil. Sulphur, iron sulphate and other acidifying agents can sometimes be added to reduce pH. Some ericaceous plants such as blueberries and rhododendrons like acid soil.

NO DIG

Wherever possible, do not dig the soil. Digging the soil will kill many of its creatures and break up the natural drainage they have created. Arable farmers have caught onto no dig (instead of ploughing), which they call minimal tillage, finding it improves soil structure, moisture retention, germination and yields, and cuts costs, weeds and fuel use.

I used to enjoy the exercise of digging. Many people don't. This method gets you out of it.

- By digging the soil you will encourage much more rapid breakdown of organic matter, which you have to replace.

- Digging the soil exposes it to erosion from rain and wind. It also increases the leaching of nitrogen and other water-soluble nutrients from the soil.

- Digging soil will bring weed seeds to the surface where they will quickly germinate and grow. Thus digging actually increases the need to weed.

Instead, mulch to stop weeds, and grow green manure cover crops to add nutrients and stop erosion.

The system of cultivation and cropping described in this book was developed by the O'Brien family, Rosa Dalziel O'Brien and her daughter Muriel and sons Kenneth and Peter, on commercial holdings in East Yorkshire, Australia and Leicester. Their rejection of the use of animal waste was based primarily on the wastes attracting soil pests, rather than avoiding exploitation of and cruelty to animals.

Geoffrey Rudd invented the term veganic as a contraction of vegetable organic to 'denote a clear distinction between conventional chemical based systems and organic ones based on animal manures', but Dalziel pioneered the practical method, with no digging at its core. In many ways, the writer Charles Dowding has taken up Dalziel's no dig mantra. Dowding says:

> 'Whenever soil is dug, loosened or turned over, it recovers from the disruption by re-covering with weed growth – both from roots of perennials and seeds of annuals. By contrast, when left uncultivated it has less need to re-cover and therefore grows less weeds.'

He advocates a thick, light-depriving mulch of organic matter or polythene to eradicate weeds, plus digging out woody weeds such as brambles. This leaves a clear patch ready to plant.

COMPOST

KENNETH DALZIEL O'BRIEN

O'Brien's 1986 book, *Veganic Gardening, the Alternative System for Healthier Crops*, was ahead of its time, yet now seems quite old-fashioned in some ways. O'Brien's practical guide to growing food without the use of brought-in animal wastes systematically explains the procedures for clearing ground.

He is big on the 'no dig', surface cultivation technique (and on using hoes and kneeling boards to plant) and the application of home-made compost for maintaining soil structure and fertility, as well as straw and mulches and herbal compost activator. Later chapters look at various crops, with instructions for sowing and any special requirements each might have. He's keen on raised beds with paths between, running north-south.

In natural ecosystems, plants feed the soil. They use the soil's nutrients, the sun and the rain to grow. Then they die and decompose with the help of micro-organisms back into the ground. Veganic growers assert that animals are not needed to 'process' plant material. They apply plant material directly or compost it to increase soil fertility. Animal manure may also contain pesticides that can kill your crops, or zoonoses that can be transmitted from animals to humans.

Too much animal manure can result in too much nitrogen, soft growth and lack of fruit. Vegetable compost tends to have a better balance of nutrients than animal manure.

Sandy and heavy soils often struggle with lack of ability to retain the moisture that is useful for plant growth. But poor soil can be improved without fear of causing extra problems by adding organic matter in the form of vegetable compost. The vegetable compost heap should be at the centre of your gardening (if not at the centre of your plot - place it at the edge).

The basis of the vegan approach is to use vegetable compost to add organic matter to the soil. That means all food scraps, and any garden arisings, plus any other material you can get hold of, for instance, throwaways from the greengrocer. Using these leftovers reduces waste, a great, positive by-product of the process.

The compost heap needs to be a mix of green and brown material so its rots well. Green is for nitrogen, brown for carbon – then you may need some added nutrients, with perhaps seaweed one of the best for veganics.

If the heap has warmth, damp and heat, then the ingredients cook. This kills off the bad organisms and leaves the perfect growing material. I'll give full instructions on how to make compost on p26, but before that you need to know why conventional composts can be bad news.

Never forget that the idea is to produce a rich humus to grow plants in. And that growing media should be made with materials you feel happy using to grow plants in. That means they will probably be organic, ethical and easily and locally-sourced.

Vegan composts are less likely to carry disease organisms. Even if heat-treated there is the possibility of bad organisms surviving in animal manures.

Soil is built by returning organic matter, through mulching, composting, or through green manures. With a 'compost tea', a fermented solution of plants, the addition of manure is made redundant.

MANURE AND PATHOGENS

Zoonoses (diseases that can be passed from animals to people) such as E. coli, campobacter, salmonella, listeria and mad cow disease (spongiform encephalopathy/ Creutzfeldt-Jakob disease) could possibly be transmitted from conventional manures and animal fertilisers to humans.

The most vulnerable are people with an impaired immune response, because of conditions such as HIV/AIDS, cancer treatment, immunosuppressive drug therapy, previous splenectomy, pregnancy, diabetes, alcoholism or chronic lung disease. Chemotherapy, surgery, or age make people vulnerable too. Direct contact with animals or animal manure could also be an important risk factor in indigenously acquired hepatitis E virus infection. These animals include horses, cats, dogs, rabbits, rats and pigs. Being a gardener with exposure to animal manure could be a risk factor.

If that's not enough reason why not to use animal manures, then consider the hormones, antibiotics, pesticides, heavy metals, GMOs, and parasites which could also move from the manures into your vegetables, then into you. Ground up live male chicks and leftover animal residues (tankage) can also go into conventional fertilisers. And, just as using land that could be grown on to produce animals to eat is inefficient and bad for the planet, recycling plant material through animals for fertiliser is non-sustainable.

Infection can occur not only as a result of tainted food crops, but also via the run off from improperly maintained compost piles contaminating water sources used for recreation, drinking and crop irrigation. Insects, birds and rodents can also spread pathogens present in fresh manure to other parts of the garden site and surrounding areas.

E. coli causes a severe bloody diarrhoea with cramps. Cow manure harbours the bacteria. Extended exposure to temperatures over 140F is required in order to ensure effective killing. Birds can pick up and spread the bacteria from compost heaps.

Salmonella is a bacterium that causes food poisoning. Up to 50 per cent of a herd or flock can be infected under intensive agricultural practices. Most infections (Salmonella serotype Enteriditis) are associated with poultry products, particularly eating under-cooked eggs. Salmonella isolates have been found to survive for up to six months in untreated cattle manure, and up to 21 days if composted.

Campylobacter jejuni cause gastrointestinal illnesses. Most cases of campylobacteriosis are from eating under-cooked poultry. The organism is present in both cattle and poultry manure.

Listeria monocytogenes are found naturally as saprophytes on decaying plant matter, as well as in soil and manure. Brucella spp. can be found in animal manure, as can Yersinia enterocolitica. And Cryptosporidium parvum and Giardia Lambila (both parasites) cause diarrhoea and may cause prolonged disease in the immunocompromised.

Salmonella isolates have been found to survive for up to six months in untreated cattle manure ...

Leaf compost.

Manure users will argue that the composting process kills pathogens because of the high temperatures it generates, but the temperatures created by the bacteria within the pile are not guaranteed through to the edges of the manure pile.

A study by John McLaughlin (Gardens as a Source of Infectious Disease: Reducing the Risk Miami Dade County Extension Service 2002) recommends:

'Do not spread raw manure on the garden. Avoid the use of animal manure when composting, particularly in a small home garden compost pile, where temperatures are unlikely to be sufficiently high to guarantee killing potential pathogens.'

Animal faecal matter that can also be zoonotic by containing round worms, hookworms, tapeworms and a variety of protozoan parasites can come from pets as well as wild animals such as foxes, as well as in manure from farm animals.

MANURE AND WEEDKILLER RESIDUE

Possibly an even bigger issue in horse manure is persistent herbicide traces. This can cause crops to yellow and die when they grow in manure produced from animals, if they have eaten fodder treated with a hormone broadleaf weedkiller chemical such as aminopyralid up to five years after treatment.

Aminopyralid and clopyralid are found in certain lawn weedkillers as well as agricultural products. In Europe, these neonicotinoid pesticides (linked to bee decline) are under severe legislative pressure. Seeds come treated with neonics and a 2013 study published in the *Journal of Applied Ecology* by Dr Dave Goulson of the University of Sussex found the soil half-life of seed treatment neonics can range from 200-1,000 days and can leach into water courses.

Silage or hay feed can pass through animals without the chemicals breaking down. The weedkiller is bound to the lignin in grass in the manure and released as undigested grass residues decay. Bracken has been linked to human gastric cancer where people, particularly children, eat dairy products where bracken has formed a significant part of cows' diet. Legionnaires' disease is also linked to shop-bought bags of compost. The University of Strathclyde carried out tests on 22 commercial brands and found evidence of the bacteria in 14 of them.

MAKING VEGETABLE COMPOST

Having looked at the reasons why not to use conventional composts, you need to know how to build the soil so plants are higher in nutrients and less likely to become diseased or attacked by insects.

The answer is to make your own compost from vegetable matter. For that you need to make a compost pile. You can also add organic vegetable matter direct by mulching the soil and letting the bacteria and organisms and worms in the soil take the nutrients down below ground. In the compost heap, this happens away from the plot.

There is no definitive way of making the compost, but here are some ideas:

• Construct two (at least) compost bays made from old pallets (see p50) placed on bare ground so worms can freely enter the cycle and fill them with plant material and turn several times a year. One can be maturing while the other one is added to. Expect fiable compost in up to four weeks (in summer – it takes a few months in winter when it is colder). You can also use hay bales with a tarpaulin cover to make a bin.

• Keep the compost bins covered, to prevent them becoming too wet, and water them during long dry spells.

• Compost old veg peelings and any plant matter you get your hands on, including grass clippings, but avoid persistent weeds such as dandelions or bindweed. Put them in a bucket of water to rot.

• Get the mix right through trial and error, with one third

HACKS/TOP TIPS TO BUILD FERTILITY

• Recycle plant material and kitchen waste to feed the soil, not the plant.

• Use green kitchen waste, grass cuttings and brown straw, paper, card.

• Retain heat in the heap with solid sides and cover the top with plastic to keep in heat and moisture or use a 'Dalek' compost bin.

• Collect and use municipal green waste/buy commercial municipal green waste.

• Make leaf mould: for soil conditioner/mulch – needs air to break down – typically in a chicken wire cage.

• Use wood chip and hedge cuttings: good for putting humus and carbon into the soil and, when rotted, can be used as potting mix and mulch.

• Sieve bought (or home-made) compost, before you use it, to get rid of lumps. This also adds air after compost compresses or soaks up water when stacked. Fluffed up material goes further, filling more pots and containers. And having more air allows roots to grow better.

brown (dry leaves/needles, wood, straw, paper), one third green (grass cuttings and garden waste), and a third from your kitchen/house (peel, hair, coffee grounds, tea, ash).

• Look at traditional gardener use of horse manure from a new angle, starting at what horses eat, rather than what they excrete: horses eat oats, which store nitrogen. They might eat alfalfa, a legume in symbiosis with rhizobium bacteria that captures nitrogen from the air. Alfalfa meal can be 6 per cent nitrogen, 4 per cent phosphorus and 2 per cent potassium. So you can make vegan compost using food horses eat, minus the hay, which, as I have mentioned, can be contaminated with weedkiller.

• Controlling the decay through the mixture of organic materials and the amount of moisture and oxygen available to the micro-organisms, which do the work of decomposition, is the art of the gardener.

Aerobic composting needs a lot of oxygen and heats the compost pile to aid decay. Issues to tackle include too slow decomposition, flies and smell, so the mix of ingredients is important. Food scraps from the kitchen, grass clippings and fresh plant matter (which are high in nitrogen) form the green material, while high in carbon materials like dry straw make up the brown matter.

Use two-thirds brown to one-third green. Turn or at least fork the pile to add air. If you don't, the pile can putrefy. But you might also need to water the pile, if it dries out, to help the decay speed up. In the winter, green material might be in short supply, so more kitchen waste would be needed. But in winter, composting is slow because of lower temperatures, and compost is not needed so much because plants aren't growing,

Bacteria and fungi feed on the fresh plant materials and break them down, using carbon in these materials to provide themselves with energy, breathing it out as carbon dioxide. They multiply, the heap heats, then as the green matter runs out, they die off. Mulching direct causes the bacteria and fungi in the soil to rot the green matter in situ.

The composting process itself can kill off plant pathogens, fungi and weed seeds if heat remains above 50°C-70°C. For the smaller space, you can have a compost bin on a balcony.

BUYING READY-MADE COMPOST

The chances are you will not be able to find enough green food scraps to make enough compost. But you should try and make as much as possible to sustain your soil. You might not have much outdoor space to make compost. Maybe you only need a bit for patio pots or for window box growing. The advantage of this is that your growing space will be close to your food scrap production space (unlike, say, the allotment).

Green waste is acceptable as an environmentally-friendly growing

(Ben Kercx Pixabay)

media, though ideally you should create a 'closed' system so you do not deplete resources from elsewhere. Green waste collected from another place should go back into that place, just as fallen leaves beneath trees should feed the trees they fell from. Decomposed leaves are a valuable and free way to help soil.

The problems for the beginner to vegan gardening are that it is difficult to find commercial vegan compost, (postage is high to buy online too) and there is a lack of awareness of vegan needs in this area (though this is lessening as vegan numbers grow). The dilemma is that natural growing media products such as peat and coir have their own environmental cost and come from outside your closed system.

If you think about being kind to the environment, that's the start to vegan gardening, same as veganism. If in doubt, then think organic, then 'super organic'.

Solutions – there are commercial products available, and companies will make bespoke mixes. Garden centres or big box-style DIY centres might sell these, as may more specialist retailers.

Beware – many conventional composts will have bonemeal in them. You will need to check the label or contact the manufacturer. It is better to make your own unless you have specialist advice that a commercial product is vegan.

When it rains, particles of peat and leaf mould wash into streams and rivers, and are then deposited

... peat would be a great, cheap growing medium – if it was not for the environmental damage it causes ...

into lakes and dams. These particles are collected and processed to produce a growing medium that is just like peat, without having to dig it up.

Moorland Gold is made by West Riding Organics from peat washed into rivers and is an environmentally acceptable retail product rich in naturally occurring minerals, as is Revive, a green waste compost.

Moorland Gold top soils are made by blending the same naturally occurring peat product with river sand.

Melcourt make a special blend for Manchester vegan outlet Hulme Community Garden Centre. The mix is based on its Soil Association-certified organic peat-free growing medium, Sylvamix Natural, but in this case Melcourt omits the organic fertiliser. This is because, although the fertiliser holds SA organic

certification, it is not free from animal-derived products. Hulme adds its own fertiliser and/or liquid feed. The basic mix includes fine composted pine bark, SA approved PAS100 certified green compost and Soil Association-approved coir. Melcourt products do not routinely contain green compost, but in the case of the Soil Association-approved mixes it benefits the balance of the recipe to achieve the required levels of efficacy for the commercial grower. One of the other aspects of producing such a mix is not what Melcourt put in but rather what they don't. By that, they mean that it is important they make sure that mixing/bagging lines are cleared prior to manufacture to avoid cross contamination with regular mixes.

Coir can be seen as a difficult choice because it takes a crop from one place where it could nurture soil and brings it a long way to another. Fertile Fibre makes a specialist vegan blend from coir. This is imported in ships from Sri Lanka. Ship miles are not as bad as road miles and air miles for the environment. In Sri Lanka and surrounding countries, there is a lot of waste coir. The company's Matthew Dent says his customers do not want to use peat because it damages the environment,

want to know what they are putting in the soil and trust what they are using, and want to avoid green waste because of its lack of traceability. They are becoming more conscious of the difference between what they can buy in garden centres and products such as his.

Fertile Fibre has been producing vegan coir compost for 20 years as part of the range and sales continue to grow. The issue with vegan Fertile Fibre is that it runs out of nitrogen quite quickly so needs a liquid feed added, for instance, from comfrey. You can use the compost for sowing seed, potting plants, seed transplants, containers and for seed germination in hydroponic systems. The product is good for water absorption. Water little and often. Ingredients are coir, vermiculite and Fertile Fibre nutrient NB5. Its Vegro potting compost also includes bark and sterilised loam.

Dent says that UK peat mining's days are numbered, but admits peat would be a great, cheap growing medium – if it was not for the environmental damage it causes. His product is mainly sold by mail order and will never be as cheap as peat-based products, he adds.

Cumbrian company Dalefoot makes bracken/wool compost. However, veganic gardeners would not use wool, because it is an animal by-product.

The brown autumn and winter bracken fronds can be rotted down in a plastic sack in the same way as autumn leaves are allowed to decompose over two years to make leaf mould. If the bracken is cut while green, rather than when it is brown in the autumn, it will

compost well when shredded.

When bracken is sporing, be careful about the carcinogenic chemical ptaquiloside. Gloves and a facemask should be worn when handling the sporing plant.

Bracken ash can also be used as a fertiliser. Left to dry and then burnt, it will produce ash with a high level of potassium and a high pH which can be used as a fertiliser. Treat as wood ashes and keep dry until required. Burning will effectively destroy any ptaquiloside and the ashes are safe.

Florablend is a recommended US vegan compost/fertiliser brand. General Hydroponics is a good source of vegan products.

Too much damp green can mean the compost mats together, going rotten and anaerobic in the absence of oxygen.

Brown materials have high carbon content and thus need nitrogen and time to break them down. So use them sparingly or on the surface of the pile.

Add in soil for its worms (don't use farmed worms) and micro-organisms, which will get things moving in the pile. Ensure the compost is ready and stable when you apply it onto the plot. Half cooked, it will use its energy composting and could burn plant roots.

WHAT TO AVOID WHEN MAKING VEGAN COMPOST
- **Animal products:** Cheese, meat, eggs. For ethical reasons, and because they attract animals such as rats.
- **Weeds that easily spread:** some weed seeds will survive the composting process e.g. dandelions.

- **Diseased plants:** better to burn them as viruses can persist.
- **Animal faeces:** brings unwanted bacteria to your compost.

WHAT OTHER ELEMENTS DOES A COMPOST HEAP NEED?
- **Carbon** – for energy; the microbial oxidation of carbon produces the heat, if included at suggested levels. High carbon materials tend to be brown and dry.
- **Nitrogen** – to grow and reproduce more organisms to oxidise the carbon. High nitrogen materials tend to be green (or colourful, such as fruits and vegetables) and wet.
- **Oxygen** – for oxidising the carbon, the decomposition process.
- **Water** – in the right amounts to maintain activity without causing anaerobic conditions.
- **Activator** – an optional high-nitrogen additive to get things going (see p55).

WHAT IS IN COMPOST THAT YOU CAN'T SEE?
- **Bacteria** – The most numerous of all the micro-organisms found in compost.
- **Actino bacteria** – Necessary for breaking down paper products such as newspaper, bark, etc.

- **Fungi, moulds and yeast** – help break down materials that bacteria cannot, especially lignin in woody material.
- **Protozoa** – Help consume bacteria, fungi and micro organic particulates.
- **Rotifers** – Rotifers help control populations of bacteria and small protozoans.

COMPOST BINS
Make a compost bin or use a commercially available Dalek-style bin. Less eco-friendly and satisfying, but enclosed, tidy, clean and handy for small spaces.

Wooden pallets compost bin: you can use three pallets screwed or tied together in a triangle, or even make a square and remove the front pallet when it's time to take out the compost. Disturbing the soil under the compost bin helps facilitate worms getting into the compost and doing their work, and also allows air flow and better drainage. You can source pallets from your local garden/ hardware/ building supplier/skip.

Other options are a few stacked tyres to put your compost in. The tyres retain heat and are easy to dismantle to get out the cooked compost.

INGREDIENTS OF VEGAN COMPOST

Brown (Carbon):

- Dry leaves
- Hay & straw
- Dried grass
- Plant stems
- Sawdust, shredded paper, cardboard
- Bits of wood, bark, nutshells and pruned twigs
- Wood ash
- Tea bags
- Coir coconut fibre
- Pine needles

Green (Nitrogen):

- Grass clippings (damp)
- Flowers and plant cuttings
- Weeds
- Vegetable and fruit leftovers/peelings
- Coffee grounds
- Hedge trimmings
- Seaweed

TRENCH COMPOSTING

Trench composting involves digging a ditch about 3ft (1m) deep and burying kitchen scraps and vegetable waste in it. Do this at any time. Starting in autumn works well for spring crops. Cover each new layer with soil. When the trench is full, wait a couple of months before sowing or planting as you would in a regular garden bed.

TURF COMPOST

If you have dug up turf, then stack squares upside down and leave them for a year. They will develop into a useful fibrous loam-type compost. The weed seeds in the turf may not decompose if you put the turf into the compost pile. Remember that the top level of turf is full of micro-organisms that like the light and nutrients within that layer. This is the basis of no dig gardening, which is a basic of soil health and has long been advocated as the best way to garden veganically.

HÜGELKULTUR

Making raised garden beds or mounds filled with rotting wood is also called Hügelkultur in German. Benefits of hügelkultur garden beds include water retention and warming of soil. Buried wood becomes like a sponge as it decomposes, able to capture water and store it for later use by crops planted on top of the hügelkultur bed. The buried decomposing wood will also give off heat, as all compost does, for several years.

BOKASHI

Bokashi is a method that uses a mix of micro-organisms to cover food waste or wilted plants to decrease smell. Bokashi in Japanese means 'shading off' or 'gradation'. The practice derives from when, centuries ago, Japanese farmers covered food waste with soil that contained the micro-organisms which would ferment the waste. After a few weeks, they would bury the waste. Use bran or sawdust which is carbon-rich plus a sugar for food such as molasses. The mixture is layered with food waste in a sealed container and, after a few weeks, removed and buried.

WOOD CHIPS

Some say to avoid wood chips as a mulch because they have too much carbon and take a long time to break down and can deprive your plants of nitrogen. I'd burn dry sticks thicker than a finger and use the ash as a soil tonic.

However, wood chip is often made up of leaves as well as bark and wood itself. There is generally too much brown to make effective compost, but if left to rot for a couple of months, then turned, it can work. Water can run straight through. The opposite effect takes place with sawdust, where water glues up the material. Wood chip does not need covering from rain and when mixed with other materials can add bulk and nutrients to compost.

It is best to layer wood chips with at least double the amount of green material. Wood chip is useful as a cover for a compost bin though to keep down smells, flies and retain heat and water.

LEAF MOULD

Decomposed leaves are a valuable and free way to help soil. Leaf mould

Clockwise from top left: sand, coir, woodchip, peat-free.

is made on a small scale by stashing leaves in a bag with holes in and leaving for a year. Rake up leaves weekly and add to the bag. When almost full, sprinkle with water, shake and tie. Use as a mulch around plants, where the black, crumbly result will decompose into the soil and add nutrients.

Roadside leaves may be contaminated with heavy metals, dog faeces and rubbish. Woodland leaves should be left to decompose so trees can take their nutrients back up to feed themselves. Parks and garden leaves are best. Thick evergreen leaves are not as good as deciduous leaves because they decompose slower. Well-rotted leaf mould is good for seed-sowing, or if mixed with sharp sand, garden compost and soil as a potting compost. Poorer leaf mould is better used just as a mulch.

HUMANURE

Vegans can use human manure or urine (produced by vegans, so it is vegan) to ensure that the nutrients they consume are given back to the soil. This ensures animal products do not go into the soil, just as non-vegan gardeners would not use meat-eating animal manure on their plots, preferring vegetarian horse or cow manure. Human wastes from vegans can also be composted and used to add organic matter to the soil.

The word humanure was promoted by Joseph Jenkins in a 1994 book about organic soil amendment. If you have a compost toilet, the products are suitable for garden use. Applying humanure direct is inadvisable.

Human urine can be added as fertiliser too because urine is high in nitrogen. The urea in urine is the end product of breakdown of proteins in the body. Urine can activate compost heaps, or, diluted, be used as a plant booster.

LOCAL AUTHORITY GREEN WASTE

Local authority green waste can be contaminated with animal manure, pathogens, heavy metals, glass and plastics as well as GMOs and radioactive material. I have visited these sites and they filter out the contaminants pretty thoroughly, however, the result is not consistent, unlike peat. Many commercial composts contain local authority green waste, but they may add animal-derived fertiliser to them. Veolia uses parks and garden waste to make Pro-Grow Soil Association-certified compost, which is vegan.

BIOCHAR

Biochar is a porous, high carbon form of charcoal used to improve soil nutrition, growing conditions and soil structure. It is made from any waste woody biomass that has been charred at a low temperature with a restricted supply of oxygen, in a process called pyrolysis. This process results in a stable form of carbon that is removed from the atmospheric carbon cycle when added as a soil amendment.

Biochar company Carbon Gold founder Craig Sams advocates pricing carbon into the cost of food, to make people farm in a different way, instead of plundering the soil's nutrients and adding them back through artificial fertilisers and tackling pests and diseases that build up in denuded soils with sprays.

This reflects the thinking of Eve Balfour, who wrote *The Living Soil* which proposed a new approach to agriculture that worked with nature. It became known as organic farming and led to the Soil Association's foundation in 1947.

Sams says more than 30 years of trials at the Rodale Institute farms in Pennsylvania show that organic farming can sequester one tonne of carbon per annum and can match industrial farming yields when the soil is rejuvenated.

Biochar is not burnt to ash but is a form of charcoal that has some of the same characteristics as humus, plus, when it is buried in the soil, it stores carbon so it doesn't enter the air as carbon dioxide and contribute to global warming.

If you add 18-20 tonnes of compost per hectare of land, only one tonne of the carbon in the compost stays in the soil. As the compost decays into humus, the rest goes off into the atmosphere as carbon dioxide. With biochar, 10-20 per cent of the carbon goes off as carbon dioxide

after a decade or so, but the rest is sequestered in the soil for hundreds if not thousands of years. One tonne of carbon locked away in biochar represents three tonnes of carbon dioxide equivalent being removed from the atmosphere.

If biochar is in the soil, it reduces nitrous oxide emissions by up to 50 per cent, because of the proliferation of soil biota that sequesters it, so farmers can halve their nitrate use and get the same results. The ancient material naturally helps improve soil structure, enhances soil fertility and increases soil health, while sequestering atmospheric carbon dioxide for hundreds of years.

COMPOST ACTIVATORS

To speed up the process there are several ways of helping the pile. The only reason to add fertiliser to a compost pile is to help feed the microbes. If your compost pile ingredients are mostly browns, there will be a deficiency of nitrogen. Adding more nitrogen will speed up composting. Good nitrogen sources include urea, grass clippings, comfrey tea leftovers, or wet nettles.

Commercially available compost accelerators/starters/activators also work. Add soil, which will add more microbes and costs nothing. In the garden centres, you can buy Garotta to speed up the process.

Some composting recipes advise you to add lime, which will raise the pH of the compost. The initial pH of garden clippings and manure will be between 5 and 7. Manure is close to seven, and woody stuff is more acidic. In the first few days of composting, acids are produced and these will lower the pH to

about 5. The acidic phase helps kill pathogens. As composting proceeds, the pH will slowly increase to a final pH of about 7 to 7.5.

GREEN MANURES

Green manures such as mustard and alfalfa add nitrogen, organic matter and soil structure, as well as protecting the soil and its moisture and keeping weeds down. Cut down before they go to seed and let the soil mulch them in, or you can hoe them in. Worms and microbes will transform hoed in green manure crops into humus.

The plants are then mixed in with the soil or could be left on the surface as a mulch. Soil analysis shows a green manure crop is the equivalent to adding about 2.5kg per square metre of farmyard manure.

Having a non-productive crop in your growing cycle may seem odd, but green manures have a long history of success in boosting the soil. The Chinese and Ancient Greeks used them several thousand years ago and today this solution to soil fertility problems is just as useful as ever.

Around 5-20g of nitrogen per square metre is produced when extracted from the air by legumes such as clovers or lupins for instance, then converted into nitrates inside the roots. Minerals that can be washed away accumulate in green manures. Crimson clover can recycle 13g of nitrogen, 6g of calcium, 1.5g of magnesium, 16g of potassium and 2g of phosphorus per square metre. Buckwheat, clover and lupins are particularly good at finding phosphorus, which helps a plant convert other nutrients into usable building blocks with which to grow.

Phosphorus is one of the main three nutrients most commonly found in fertilisers and is the 'P' in the NPK balance that is listed on fertilisers.

HACKS

Plant red or white clover over winter, which fixes nitrogen from the air and brings up minerals from the ground, as well as stopping bare soil eroding. Plant as a cover crop, and as an under sown crop. Rake in two weeks before planting potatoes.

In the spring, plant trefoils, crimson or sweet clover, mustard, buckwheat or phacelia. Vetch, lucerne, mustard, buckwheat, phacelia and red and white clover are also good for autumn planting.

Top row: green manure seeds, ready to sow. bottom row: sowing, the results of sowing green composts between crops.

FERTILISERS

F eed vegan plants too for better yields and health, by using a vegan compost tea, or rock dust. Take a pre-emptive strike. It's like eating well for health, rather than taking medicine. Plants need nitrogen (N), phosphorous (P) and potassium (K). NPK is the chemical basis of garden fertilisers.

Organic gardeners build fertility through crop rotation using nitrogen fixing crops like legumes, seaweed extracts and rotted plants such as comfrey and nettles. Plants also need sulphur, magnesium, iron, cobalt, boron, molybdenum, copper and zinc. A liquid kelp fertiliser can boost deficiencies.

Apply fertilisers as mulch, liquid feeds or foliage sprays. Starving plants need more NPK. Lack of nitrogen is typified by pale leaves and stunted plants. Lack of

Organic/green controls and supplements.

phosphate is shown by poor root development. Potassium or potash deficiency causes scorched leaves and poorly coloured veg and fruit. Lack of magnesium, manganese and iron leads to yellow or brown patches between veins. Well-fed plants are better able to resist pests and diseases. Too much animal manure can result in too much nitrogen, soft growth and lack of fruit. Vegetable compost tends to have a better balance of nutrients than animal manure. Ideally, top dress with vegetable compost in spring.

As discussed, the conventional wisdom is blood, fish and bone are the best way to add the nitrogen, potassium, and phosphorus to the soil. These elements all come from the plants that the animals ate first, so cut out the middleman, and the by-products of abattoirs.

Many plants will grow with little attention. Rhubarb, asparagus, artichokes, potatoes, onions, tree fruit, bush fruit, beetroot and kale are all examples of crops that are pretty fool-proof. Feed them too for better yields and health, but with a vegan compost tea or rock dust.

Buying vegan compost or fertiliser is now an option. Neudorff sells vegan organic orchid feed which has an NPK of 3-1.5-5 and is made with the natural fermentation by-product of processing sugar beet – vinasse.

Euromonitor retail analyst Damian Shore has suggested there is a gap in the market for vegetarian fertiliser:

'Increased interest in vegetarian and vegan diets, particularly among younger consumers, combined with the growing popularity of urban gardening and (to a lesser extent) the trend towards pet humanisation, suggests there is some potential in this area.'

In April 2013, Neudorff launched Azet Veggie Fertiliser. It uses 100 per cent plant-based raw materials. The product targets vegan organic food production.

COMFREY

Comfrey is good at sucking up nutrients from the soil and contains calcium, phosphorus, potassium, vitamin A, C and other trace materials.

Grow comfrey by, with permission, digging up a bit of someone's crop. When divided it grows again easily and produces leaf rapidly. You can buy root cuttings to plant from May-September.

Make a comfrey liquid feed by filling a container with leaves and topping up with water. Leave to steep for a week and pour the liquid onto crops. Then add the used

Comfrey, the basis of making natural fertiliser. Just steep in a bucket of water and pour on your plants.

Harvest (left). Stirring comfrey fertiliser (right).

comfrey (or use fresh) to the compost pile, where its nutrients will both enrich the whole heap and encourage decomposition. Also, add to leaf mould to make richer compost. Comfrey has a high carbon to nitrogen ratio.

Other uses are to spread leaves as a mulch to slow evaporation of moisture, suppress weeds, enrich the soil as it rots and distract slugs and snails from your crops. You can lay a layer of wilted comfrey in the trench before planting potatoes.

OTHER FERTILISER PLANTS
Similar plants to comfrey with similar uses:

- **Nettle:** vitamins A, C, and K, calcium, magnesium, phosphate, phosphorus, potassium, boron, bromine, copper, iron, selenium and zinc.
- **Parsley:** vitamins A and C, iron, copper and manganese.
- **Dandelion:** vitamins A and C, calcium and potassium.
- **Stinging Nettle:** magnesium, sulphur and iron.
- **Horsetail:** silica.

MYCORRHIZA
Mycorrhizal fungi form large networks of fine growth throughout the soil where plant roots grow. They associate with most types of plant roots and act in the same way as roots, collecting water and nutrients such as phosphorus and potassium for the plants. In return the leaves of plants send sugars to the fungi. You can add bought mycorrhiza to sterile or bare soil.

ROCK DUST
Volcanic rock dust is like a vitamin pill for the garden. The natural minerals speed up the composting process and adds minerals to the compost. Rock dust is up to 400 million years old, when vertebrate life had not yet evolved. Basalt-based volcanic rock dust or lava dust comes from magma, from the centre of the Earth, rather than from any human or animal input.

Remin, a Scottish company, has researched modern usage of rock dust. The theory is plants suck minerals out of the soil, slowly depleting these ancient reserves. NPK are easy to find, but minerals like calcium and trace elements like iron and manganese can be tough to replace once they're depleted, so rock dust can be a useful addition to compost or soil.

COMPOST TEA
The crossover between compost and fertiliser is compost tea. Vegan compost tea is a perfect substitute for fertiliser, which will probably not be organic – or vegan.

Compost teas and mycorrhiza are increasingly better understood elements of soil health. To make compost tea, soak a porous bag of compost in a bucket of water, then aerate it, to create a liquid fertiliser, full of micro-organisms. This tea goes beyond liquid fertiliser made by soaking comfrey or nettles in water, as its microbes compete against disease organisms in plants.

Use mature, aged compost that will break down easily. The most decomposed from the bottom of the pile is best. Fill a bucket 1/3 full of mature vegan compost. Top up with water. Steep for three days. Strain through a sack or any fabric. Dilute the remainder 1:10 with water. Return the solids left to the compost. Pour the tea onto your plants. The result will be increased plant growth thanks to the nutrients added to the plant via soil, via the tea.

ALTERNATIVE FERTILISER METHODS

FOREST GARDENING

Forest gardening takes an ecosystem approach to gardening. It makes use of vertical space by growing multiple layers of plants in the same area; a canopy of fruit or nut trees can have understories of edible shrubs, herbs, vegetables, berries, roots and fungi, and as well as supporting fertility plants.

PERMACULTURE

Permaculture is based on sustainability, and designing gardens, farms and settlements to meet the needs of the earth and humans in the long term. In permaculture, people imitate natural ecosystems by observing the world and applying ecological principles to garden layouts.

Permaculture is an ecosystem to produce crops thanks to the relationships between its layered trees, understorey, ground cover, soil, fungi and insects. The top layer is large trees, then dwarf trees, berry bushes, herbs/leaf veg, 'rhizosphere' root veg and mycorrhizal, surface (e.g. strawberries) and vertical vines.

Biodynamics involves integrating soil fertility, plant growth and livestock, adding spiritual and mystical ideas and using manures and no artificial chemicals on soil and plants. Part of the system is

Plants get energy from the sun, but the theory suggests they are also affected by the moon, just as tides are ...

gardening at night by the phases of the moon to produce better veg. You need a moon timetable to tap into the energy cycles of the moon and harness its lunar energy.

The philosophy was founded in 1924 by Austrian teacher and philosopher Rudolf Steiner to use holistic principles and take into account the condition of the cosmos. Plants get energy from the sun, but the theory suggests they are also affected by the moon, just as tides are. The moon's pull causes high tides twice a month, a day after full and new moons. This leads to rainfall peaking three or four days after full and new moons, say moon gardeners. Plant pumpkins three days before a full moon, according to Native American tradition.

There is some scientific evidence behind the method; gardeners at RHS Wisley in the UK have proved the benefits of the lunar effect under controlled research conditions, with increased yields of 20-30 per cent. The system has a lot in common with veganic gardening and includes the use of cover crops, green manures and crop rotation.

Apart from lunar gardening, methods unique to the biodynamic approach include a closed system of composting from your own animals and the use of fermented herbal and mineral preparations as compost additives and field sprays, as well as using the astronomical sowing and planting calendar.

Some aspects of conventional biodynamics (which is non-vegan) include horn-manure, a mixture prepared by filling the horn of a cow with cow manure and burying it in the autumn to decompose during the winter and recover for use the following spring, diluted one teaspoon with 50 litres of water. Biodynamicists also put crushed powdered quartz into a buried horn in spring and take it out in autumn. They mix one tablespoon of quartz powder to 250 litres of water and spray on crops to prevent fungal diseases. Yarrow blossom in buried red deer bladders, chamomile blossoms in buried cow's small intestines and oak bark buried inside animal skulls are other biodynamic ways.

Vegan gardeners would use tree bark sheaths instead to hold preparations such as crushed quartz to bury, dig up and then make fertiliser spray. Herbs you can bury in the sheath include yarrow, camomile, nettles, chopped oak bark, dandelion, valerian and horsetail.

BIOINTENSIVE

Gardener and researcher John Jeavons developed the biointensive approach to grow green with high yields. You double-dig, so root systems can go deeper. Plants are grown densely. No animals are reared. The plants grown are meant to meet year-round nutritional needs. In this calorie farming method, you grow enough food for energy and nutrients to live on in a minimal area. Root crops such as potatoes, sweet potatoes, garlic, leeks, burdock, Jerusalem artichoke and parsnips are often used in calorie farming because they allow biointensive farmers and gardeners to grow more yield, calories and nutrients in smaller areas, resulting in less labour per calorie, and more space for wilderness and people.

LASAGNE GARDENING/SHEET COMPOSTING

In lasagne gardening, also known as sheet composting, layers of organic matter are piled on the surface of the ground. This is a no dig method. Several layers of cardboard are placed directly on the lawn. Layers of organic matter are added on top, alternating between layers of brown leaves, small twigs, newspaper, cardboard, and layers of green fruit and veg scraps, grass clippings, and weeds that haven't gone to seed. Initially stacked 60cm high, the materials decompose in place, shrinking down and creating a fertile medium for gardening. If you have enough organic matter available, this is an option for gardening on hard surfaces.

SELF-FERTILISING GARDENS

This method involves permanent raised beds, permanent ground cover, surface composting, a diversity of plants in each bed, the presence of living perennial roots at all times and using height with climbing plants. Biomass from leaves and stalks are left directly on the surface to decompose, and roots are left to decompose naturally underground. The principle elements of self-fertilising gardens are raised beds, water points, and trees, and the interconnection between these elements. The aim is to create a dynamic ecosystem that self-fertilises.

JAPANESE NATURAL AGRICULTURE

Japanese natural agriculture was developed in Japan independently of international influences. Most practitioners use entirely plant-based techniques. Church of World Messianity spiritual leader Mokichi Okada came up with a no-fertiliser technique in the 1930s, which he later named nature farming. It differs from typical organic agriculture in two main ways: the crops are not rotated, and it is considered part of a spiritual pursuit for beauty and peace. A separate branch of Japanese natural farming was developed by farmer and philosopher Masanobu Fukuoka, author of *The One Straw Revolution* (1975). He was a proponent of no-till methods for growing grains and vegetables.

SQUARE FOOT GARDENING

Square foot gardening involves an open-bottomed box, divided into a grid, that is filled with a mix of light soil and compost. Each section in the grid is one square foot. Each square foot contains the optimum number of plants, depending on the space that the plant takes up, and companion plants are often planted in the same square. Once planted, there is less weeding and watering than with typical gardens. This technique is an option for urban gardens and for people with reduced mobility, as it can be built on a table top.

BIODIVERSITY

Wild areas will encourage beneficial wildlife and insects to come to your plot. They will prey on 'pests' that might eat your crops. Hoverflies eat greenfly. Ground beetles and amphibians eat slugs. So leave wilder areas, grow a berry hedge which encourages birds which will prey on slugs, under plant the hedge with wildflowers. Leave beetle banks and nettle patches. To encourage butterflies and bees, have a pond with flowering plants such as flag iris and water lily. Flowers to use in vegetable gardens include calendula and nasturtiums which attract insects that eat pests and insects that pollinate.

The aim is to attract hoverflies, lacewings, ladybirds and others that eat aphids, mites, thrips, mealybugs and scale insects and to attract pollinating bees, wasps, hoverflies, moths, butterflies and certain species of beetle.

Try calendula pot marigolds and French marigolds, chamomile and daisy, poached egg plants, alliums, umbellifers, comfrey, nasturtium and the green manure plants phacelia, buckwheat, and clover. You can also buy ready-made wildflower meadow mixes which use both annual and perennial mixes to prolong flowering time or you can also buy the seeds separately and mix them yourself. You need 1g per square metre of pure wildflower seeds and 5g per square metre of grass and wildflower meadow seeds.

GROW TO EAT

GETTING STARTED

If you are growing and eating veganically, the best crops to grow are the ones that have lots of calcium, vitamin D, zinc, and protein, which non-vegans get from meat and dairy. If you are meat and dairy-free, you will need a vitamin B12 supplement as B12 isn't in non-animal foods that are not fortified.

Fruit and vegetables are the mainstays of growing your own and I detail a recommended selection below A-Z. Grains, nuts and seeds are all growable too. An adult needs about 50g of protein a day (known as the recommended daily allowance RDA), and half that or less for children. Grain such as wheat, oat, barley and rye are sources. Realistically, you aren't going to grow these at home; try quinoa.

Pulses are growable sources of protein – grow peas and beans.

Nuts are full of protein, zinc, calcium, omega-3 fatty acids, and vitamin E. A nut tree is there forever and needs little maintenance.

Seeds are great sources-for instance sunflower, pine nuts and pumpkin.

Potatoes have a bit of protein. Complete proteins contain a sufficient amount of all nine essential amino acids. Non-meat and dairy examples of protein-rich foods include quinoa, buckwheat, hemp, chia and soy.

ROTATION

Rotation is moving plants around the garden because different plants use different minerals. This will also stop the build-up of pests and diseases in the soil. Crop rotation helps stop one weed predominating. Ridged soil can be brought up to smother weeds between plants in the row. You can also hand weed.

The system is about optimising fertility and not using inputs from outside. Ideally, it's a ring-fenced system and makes most use of the land available to grow food and not depend on livestock inputs that use a lot of land so has biodiversity benefits. It keeps nutrients in.

Ideally, clear the area you want to grow on, leaving wild edges. Plant a cover crop such as trefoil or clover.

YEAR ONE

IS TYPICALLY a potato year. This breaks up the soil and makes use of the fertility fixed by the cover crop – potatoes need plenty of feeding.

Buy chitted sprouting potatoes a few weeks before planting and plant 10cm deep with the sprouting end upwards in March after frosts have finished, two weeks after raking in your cover crop.

Earth up by raking soil up over the sides of shoots to stop frost damage and harvest 3 weeks after flowering, about 10 weeks after planting.

YEAR TWO

AFTER A WINTER cover crop, is typically peas and legumes such as beans and peas, and mange tout.

Plant two runner bean seeds per cane under a wigwam of eight canes. Climbing French beans need similar support. Grow in a pot first and place outside to harden off a week before planting in the soil.

YEAR THREE

PLANT BRASSICAS such as broccoli and kale, which need slightly less nutrition. Brussel sprouts and cabbage are part of this group and grow well into winter.

Net to protect from pigeons and fleece (horticultural, wool fleece) to keep off cabbage white butterflies.

Grow lettuce and radish in between rows. Plant kale seeds outside 1cm deep from March. Plant broccoli seed out from April, 2cm deep, 15cm apart.

YEAR FOUR

PLANT ROOTS like carrots, which can suck up nutrition from deeper underground. Beetroot, chard, onion, leek and celeriac are in this group. Sow onions direct or from sets.

Sow carrot seed outdoors thinly because if you thin out to let the best seedling grow, carrot fly will smell them and eat them. Use mesh or a tall crop around carrots to put off flies.

ROTATION ON LARGER PLOTS

A seven-year rotation is a good idea on field-sized plots when using stock-free techniques. Moving the crop on helps control disease build-up and varies the plants that take nutrients in smaller or lesser amounts from the soil.

Building fertility with green manures is even more important here as large inputs required for soil fertilisation are a bigger and more financially and environmentally costly job. These inputs have to come from somewhere else, depleting that area's fertility.

Ideally Lucerne and clover as a cover crop for two years. This puts organic material back into the soil. Red clover's long tap roots of two metres break up the soil and allow earthworms to continue the task and introduce air, while bringing nutrients down into the earth. Millions of microfauna help the process of releasing nutrients.

Seven year rotation:
Two years' green manure.

Then plant potatoes which need a lot of nutrients, then green manure with another clover cover crop that winter. Don't leave soil uncovered to degrade and erode.

Plant brassicas in year four's spring.

You can then plant a winter crop of sprouting broccoli, winter cabbage, Brussel sprouts, or cauliflower.

Year five is for onions/leeks – alliums. Brassicas inhibit diseases that the onion family might get. Grow alliums from seed and transplant into the field, or onions from sets planted in biomulch made from corn starch. Grow clover between the onions.

Year six, root veg – carrot, parsnip, celeriac, beetroot, which can grow at lower fertility levels. They have long roots and open up the ground to bring nutrients and water up.

Year seven, squash and sweet corn. Squash and pumpkins store well over winter. Under the squash, grow a green manure of red clover, or lucerne. They also give weed control and get an early start on adding fertility back to the soil. Then sow

more, because you are back to year one and two.

What to grow often depends on how much space you've got. Grow fruit trees if you have a big plot and microgreens if you have a windowsill. Sprouting seeds work well in the windowsill. Remember growing cress at school on cotton wool? This is growing 101. Sprout mung beans, chickpeas, alfalfa and fenugreek on the windowsill.

NUTRITION

It pays to know what nutrients are in what you are going to grow. This helps balance your diet.

We all know bad fat, salt, sugar, idleness and processed foods are bad. Generally, a super organic vegan diet and lifestyle is good. Not supporting environmentally wasteful (and cruel) animal farming is good for the planet.

Pretty much everything that has to do with livestock puts humans and our environment at risk: animal waste; hormones; antibiotics; pesticides and fertilisers; chemicals from tanneries and other by-products that pollute water.

A vegan diet consists of bright fruit and vegetable perfect for showing off on Twitter, Facebook and Instagram. Celebrities have warmed to the diet and lifestyle. Some 16 per cent of people say they have followed celeb vegans to change their diet, say surveys. There are 54 per cent who change for ethical reasons though, after watching films like *Cowspiracy* and *Forks over Knives*. Cost is a driver too. In recession, people buy less meat. In 2008 in the UK 11.5 per cent less meat sold as UK GDP fell by one percentage point.

Veg, fruit, legumes, and grains offer plenty of antioxidants too, so health-wise, plant-based diets get a tick. Then there's the improvement in heart health, the phytochemicals, extra fibre, low saturated fat, healthy fats, hypertension dodging, weight-gain avoiding, anti-cancer, anti-diabetes nature of this diet.

There was little understanding of nutrition compared to today before the Second World War and its dig for victory ethos, which made many people think more deeply about diet. Veganism and organic farming developed at this time. In very recent years, an explosion in vegan cook books, eating out, supermarket options, and understanding, makes change easy.

Modern factory farming abuses of animals makes the need for change more pressing. Hair shirt vegans can be pretty boring, proselytising about their superior eating habits. Or to most people, difficult eating habits. As a teen veggie, pub restaurants used to offer me egg and chips or elderly crusty veg lasagne. Vegans were into wholefood 'ethnic'.

The pioneering health food Cranks restaurant in Soho, London, opened my eyes to a better way of eating – fresher, in more exotic Mediterranean and Moroccan styles, healthier. The trouble with vegan food, is it's so worthy. Dirty potatoes, brown food for green people. The humble carrot, the unassuming soy bean- the vegan's best friend. The amazing array of fruit and veg choices available today. Vegan food is now developing into convenience, after the rationing of the staples, then the exotic overseas influences. I just like normal food, like chips. Veganism, as it is known today, originated in the Second World War. Rationing and growing your own meant people once again went back to a basic diet of British produce, with a lack of meat, dairy, eggs and sugar.

Advances in science and less time to cook meant junk food and convenience recipes came in during the 1950s. You could argue it has been downhill ever since. However, advances in nutritional science mean people understand much more about their diet now. Grow your own boomed in the 1970s and 2000s,

After many years of doubt, nutritionists now realise a home-grown diet can almost completely meet nutrient needs ...

led by an oil crisis and recession respectively, and resulted in a greater understanding of how a return to a more natural way of life could combat modern health crises such as diabetes and obesity.

Back in the eighteenth century, sailors got scurvy from lack of vitamin C, prompting the start of study into nutritional science. After many years of doubt, nutritionists now realise a home-grown diet can almost completely meet nutrient needs. Vegans and vegetarians should eat 8-10 servings of fruit and veg a day. This includes a tennis ball sized bit of fruit, golf ball sized amount of dried fruit, half a tennis ball of green or root veg and a cereal bowl full of salad veg. Salad veg evidently can't be measured in sports ball sizes. But they can be grown in beach ball sizes.

Put together this gives you beta carotene (to make vitamin A), vitamins B2, B3, B5, B6, B9 (folate), vitamin C, vitamin E and vitamin K. Then there are minerals and trace elements such as calcium, iodine, iron, magnesium, manganese, phosphorus and potassium. Fruit juice counts as one portion, even if you drink a gallon.

You also need 2-3 servings of pulses such as peas, beans and lentils,

nuts or seeds (a serving is a small handful). Or two tablespoons of nut butters (a bit messy as a handful). This provides vitamins B1, B2, B3, B5, B6 and B9 and trace elements/minerals calcium, copper, iron, magnesium, manganese, phosphorus, potassium, selenium and zinc.

Added to that are 3-4 servings of pastas, bread, rice, oats, rye, buckwheat, etc (all as brown as possible). These are harder to grow in the garden. As are the vegetable oils such as flax, hemp, rape, vegetable and olive that give vitamin E and omega 3 and 6. And B12, which you can only get from fortified plant milk, yeast extract or breakfast cereal. And a litre of water a day, which you can get from the tap.

This diet will lower your fat. Three-quarters of calories from cheddar cheese comes from fat and two-fifths from salmon and roast chicken. Beat acne, heart disease, diabetes, obesity, cancer, osteoporosis and feeling bad about being mean to animals by switching to veg only.

American dietician Jack Norris says vegans should concentrate on nine nutrients: protein, zinc, calcium, iodine, iron, vitamins B12, A and D, and alpha-linolenic acid. The rest of the 40 essential nutrients are taken for granted. Most will be in what you eat, whatever you eat, without having to worry about them. However, vegans have to be aware of several potential deficiencies.

Avoid calcium deficiency by consuming calcium-rich foods such as legumes, nuts and seeds, squash, kale, sweet potato, broccoli (plus tofu made with calcium sulphate) mean you can have a super organic

vegan home grown diet. Legumes such as beans, peas, lentils and soya are protein-rich. If you can, grow and eat these.

B12 is essential for brain, nerve, and blood cell functioning and development. Vegans have to take B12 supplements, and to be more aware of their nutrient intake than omnivores. Most commercially-available soya milk is fortified with B12. Vitamin B12 is found naturally, in meat, fish, and dairy products. If you don't have enough iron, your body can't make enough healthy oxygen-carrying red blood cells.

Good plant sources of iron include:

Lentils, chickpeas, beans, tofu, cashew nuts, chia seeds, ground linseed, hemp seeds, pumpkin seeds, kale, dried apricots and figs, raisins, quinoa, dried seaweed, spirulina, potatoes, spinach, Jerusalem artichokes, and fortified breakfast cereal and fermented foods such as tempeh.

Add vitamin C to help absorb the iron. Don't drink tea when eating iron sources because it stops uptake.

A zinc deficiency can weaken the immune system and slow wound healing. It may also cause tiredness. Sources of zinc include:

Beans, chickpeas, lentils, tofu, walnuts, cashew nuts, chia seeds, ground linseed, hemp seeds, pumpkin seeds, wholemeal bread, sea veg and quinoa.

Women need 7mg a day and men 9.5mg.

Iodine is an essential nutrient. To boost iodine, sea veg is a good source. Green seaweeds, such as sea

Cows and gorillas and vegan bodybuilders grow big and strong from eating plants ...

lettuce, mainly contain chlorophyll. Red or purple seaweeds include dulse, laver, nori, agar, and Irish moss. Brown seaweeds are kelp, kombu, alaria, arame, wakame, sea palm, and hijiki. As well as being an iodine rich food, seaweed is great as a fertiliser.

Calcium intake is about how much you absorb rather than how much you eat. Soaking, sprouting, and fermenting helps. Beans, pulses and dry figs are all good sources.

Protein levels should be satisfactory in a vegan diet including foods such as beans, lentils, tempeh, natto, spirulina, amaranth, quinoa, sauerkraut, kimchi, coconut milk yoghurt, kombucha, miso, pickles and kefir.

Vitamin A in its complete form, retinol, is only found in animal products. However, the precursors to vitamin A are found in a plethora of fruits and vegetables including carrots, mango, spinach and sweet potatoes. When we eat foods containing these precursors, such as beta-carotene, our body converts them to vitamin A.

Omega-3 and 6 fatty acids (alpha-linoleic and linoleic acids) are mostly found in fatty fish, which may have the added 'bonus' of having poisonous mercury in them. But they are also in seeds and nut and soya oils and are necessary for proper brain function, health, and development.

You also need vitamin D from the sun and to be active and to be at a healthy weight. These you can get from gardening. Humans also need to feel a sense of well-being. This comes from believing you are doing your bit for the environment, and the satisfaction of making a difference.

Nutritionist Christine Bailey says you can have a healthy or unhealthy vegan diet, depending on your processed food intake. She says the biggest reason people go to the doctor is about gut health. Eating fresh and pickled/fermented fruit and veg is good for your guts. Dairy and meat generally isn't.

Canadian Dr Tushar Mehta, who has a strong interest in the medical evidence regarding plant-based diet and health, says it is 'very easy to get everything you need from a vegan diet'. Mehta's advice is to include all food groups: protein, wholegrains, fruit, veg, nuts and seeds, healthy fats; to supplement B12; and to be aware of iodine levels (iodised salt is an option), iron, calcium and protein. Plants are complete sources of protein, not incomplete as once thought. Cows and gorillas and vegan bodybuilders grow big and strong from eating plants.

Dr Mehta says soya is a 'superfood', which reduces the risk of diabetes, cuts cholesterol, and boosts brain blood vessels. He says fat vegans eat too many carbohydrates and need to replace them with beans and wholegrains. Skinny vegans need to drink vegan smoothies made from hemp seed or peanut butter.

VITAMINS AND EASILY GROWABLE CROPS YOU MIGHT GET THEM FROM:

- A-carrots, green leafy plants, broccoli, spinach, apricots, peppers, tomatoes, green herbs.
- B1-3 and B6-green leafy veg, nuts, seeds, bean sprouts, beans.
- C-fresh fruit and veg such as

UK GOVERNMENT GUIDELINES:
19-64 year old M/F
Vitamin A (µg/day) 600/700
Thiamin (mg/day) 0.8/1.0
Riboflavin (mg/day) 1.1/1.3
Niacin equivalent (mg/day) 31.2-16.5
Vitamin B (mg/day) 1.2-1.4
Vitamin B12 (µg/day) 1.5
Folate (µg/day) 200
Vitamin C (mg/day) 40
Vitamin D (µg/day) 10

Government recommendations for energy, macronutrients, salt and dietary fibre 19-64 years
Energy (MJ/day) 8.4/10.5
Energy (kcal/day) 2000/2500
Macronutrients
Protein (g/day) 45/55.5
Fat (g/day) [Less than] 78/97
Saturated fat (g/day) [Less than] 24/31
Polyunsaturated fat (g/day) 14/18
Monounsaturated fat (g/day) 29/36
Carbohydrate (g/day) [At least] 267/333
Free sugars (g/day) [Less than] 27/33
Salt (g/day) [Less than] 6.0
Dietary fibre (g/day) 30

Government recommendations for minerals for males and females aged 19-64 years
Iron (mg/d) 8.7-14.8
Calcium (mg/day) 700
Magnesium (mg/day) 270/300
Potassium (mg/day) 3500
Zinc (mg/day) 7-9.5
Copper (mg/day) 1.2
Iodine (µg/day) 140
Selenium (µg/day) 60-75
Phosphorus (mg/day) 550
Chloride (mg/day) 2500
Sodium (g/day) 2.4

leafy greens, broccoli, tomatoes, peas, citrus, bell peppers, kiwis.
- D- sunshine.
- E- nuts, seeds and pulses.
- K-dark green veg, sprouts, cauliflower, tomatoes, seaweed.
- Calcium- kale, broccoli, spinach, almonds, hazelnuts, beans.
- Iodine- green leafy veg, seaweed.
- Iron-from dark green veg, beans, pulses, almonds, herbs, figs, apricots, seeds, parsley.
- Magnesium - from green leafy veg, broccoli, almonds.
- Phosphorus, sulphur and potassium from beans, peas, seeds, potatoes, fruit and veg, nuts.
- Zinc from seeds, nuts.
- Plus fluorine, copper, cobalt, chromium, manganese, beta-carotene, sodium chloride, salt, selenium, molybdenum.

KITCHEN ESSENTIALS.
Many of these can be grown at home.
- Breakfast cereals
- Bulk whole grains: Brown rice, millet, quinoa, amaranth, barley, oats, bulgur couscous, quinoa, millet
- Pasta
- Flour
- Cornmeal polenta
- Bread
- Beans: Adzuki, black, black-eyed peas, chickpeas, kidney, butter, split peas, lima, pinto, mung, and soya. And baked, dried and tinned.
- Lentils: Brown, green, red, or yellow
- Tofu
- Tempeh
- Miso paste
- Soya sauce

- Frozen: Spinach, berries, edamame, broccoli, beans, peas, and lentils
- Nuts: Almonds, cashews, walnuts, and pecans
- Seeds: Sesame, sunflower, pumpkin, and flax
- Sea vegetables: Arame, kelp/kombu, dulse
- vegetable stock, sea salt, and black pepper
- herbs and spices
- margarine, virgin olive oil, veg oils
- vinegar
- condiments
- agar
- vegemite
- peanut butter
- crackers
- tinned veg
- coconut milk
- soya milk
- tahini
- dried fruit
- vegan mayo
- vegan chocolate
- baking powder
- sugar (alternatives include agave, maple syrup, panela, jiggery, fructose, dextrose, turbinado, cane juice). Bone char may be used to whiten cane (but not beet) sugar.
- beverages
- yeast flakes
- vegan cheese
- jam
- iodised salt
- ice cream
- frozen veg and fruit
- peanut butter, yeast extract, jam, oven chips, coconut milk, lots of curry pastes, many breakfast cereals, soy sauce, hummus, fruit juice, fizzy drinks, tea and coffee, many biscuits, crackers, crispbreads and crisps, and of course fruit

and vegetables – fresh, dried and frozen.

WHAT TO GROW

It's quite easy to grow many plants. It's quite difficult to raise meat to eat. Taking control of your diet and lifestyle begins here.

Growing super organic veganic is just the same as conventional growing in most ways. Start off with seeds, bulbs, tubers, bushes and trees. Sow or plant them in the right place at the right time. Pot on seedlings, then plan out in prepared soil. Water and feed. Harvest. Repeat.

GROWING IN CONTAINERS

Select your pot. Make sure it has drainage holes. Add some bits of crock to help drainage. Place on a stand. Sterile, sieved bark-based or loam-based compost is best. Plant your plant or seed. Mulch the top with bark to retain water. Feed and water as pots dry out and the compost will run out of nutrients.

Grow root crops such as beetroot in shallower compost, and plant potatoes and carrot deeper. Choose compact bush courgettes and tumbling

tomatoes. Peppers, chillies, strawberries and herbs are good options.

Indoors, the general rule is to sow, thin, then 'prick out' to transplant into bigger pots, then 'harden off' by introducing a cooler climate if you are going to plant the crops outside. Many plants staying indoors need lots of heat. This means using a greenhouse or propagator. Aubergines, peppers, cucumbers, melons and tomatoes need 20°C to germinate. When established, plant them in bigger pots at slightly lower temperatures.

KIT

You need less than you think. I rely on a rake, hoe, trowel, fork and spade. You also need pots, which are easy to find kicking about for free. Garden centres often give them away or make pots from empty toilet or paper towel rolls, newspaper, paper coffee cups and cereal boxes. Avoid plastic pots. Use galvanised metal or terracotta.

Make seed trays from low-sided cardboard boxes or disposable plastic food containers. Make a compost bay or use a 'Dalek' bin, which councils often supply.

A greenhouse and shed are useful for storage and year-round growing, as are cloches, while fleece protects from frosts. Net to protect from birds. Mesh to protect from insects. Secateurs are very helpful for pruning. A watering can, bucket and hose can help too.

Think about growing in containers, window boxes, patio, vertical space (up walls). 🌿

A-Z WHAT TO GROW/COOK

When talking about growing edible plants, I see it as important to include the holistic picture; nutritional benefits, and cooking, eating and drinking ideas. There are hundreds of fruit, veg, seeds, nuts and other food items you can grow, but I've chosen veg and fruit that are most nutritious and are possible to produce for the non-expert. I've picked out any higher levels of minerals, vitamins and other nutrients that they offer.

I use US nutritionist Jack Norris' nine nutrients: protein, zinc, calcium, iodine, iron, vitamins B12, A and D, and alpha-linolenic acid. There are 40 essential nutrients and I select some if they are at a high level. Then I give an easy way to prepare, cook and eat the fruit or veg, completing the how to grow-why it's good for you-how to eat it circle.

Nutrients are listed per 100g unless stated otherwise.

APPLES

The staple fruit crop. Holds a special place in my heart, because I'm an Appleby – Norse for apple farm. For a 200g apple:

NUTRITION

· Vitamin C 8mg (10%-plus of daily allowance)
· Fibre 4g
· Carbohydrates 25g
· Apples also contain trace minerals.

GROW

Think about tree size to fit your plot. Trees are grafted onto roots, which are given numbers to differentiate them by size.

· A dwarf tree (M9, G11 rootstock)
· Semi-dwarf (e.g. M26, G202, G935 rootstock)
· Semi-vigorous (e.g. MM106, M7, G30 rootstock)
· Full-size (e.g. M25, B118 rootstock)

Buy in a container or bare root. Plant dormant bare roots in autumn/early winter and containers anytime.

Plant the tree in a sunny and sheltered place. Dig a hole a third wider than the roots and to the same depth as the tree's roots, firming the bottom of the hole into a slight mound. Stick in your tree. Stake if you like. Backfill with soil.

If you're growing your tree in a container, half fill a large tub with soil-based potting compost and place your tree on top. Fill the tub with more soil to the base of the tree, water well and feed regularly.

In October, apply grease bands 45cm up the trunk to stop wingless female moths crawling up, where their caterpillars will eat fruit.

EAT

Juicing: Crush using a crushing machine or freeze and thaw apples then pound with a wooden post in a large bucket. Then use a fruit press. Keeps in the fridge for 2/3 days. Or freeze. 2.5kg of apples = 1 litre of apple juice. A mature apple tree can yield 20kg of apples a year, with an average apple weighing 150g.

Cider: Wash, chop and pulp fruit. You can use a food processor. Use a fruit press to extract the juice. Pour into

Caption to say what this is...

- Vitamin C 11.7milligram (mg) 20%
- Fibre   5.4g   14% RDA
- Vitamin K   14.8 µg   12%
- Copper   0.231 mg   27%
- Iron   1.28 mg   16%
- Magnesium   60 mg   15%
- Manganese   0.256 mg   11%
- Phosphorus   90 mg   13%

Jerusalem per 100g:
- Folates 13   µg 3%
- Vitamin C   4mg 7%
- Riboflavin   4.5%
- Thiamin   17%
- Potassium   429mg 9%
- Iron   3.4mg 42.5%
- Copper   0.14mg 15%

GROW

Globe artichokes need a sunny, sheltered site with well-drained, moisture-retentive soil to which you have added organic matter. Buy pot grown plants or sow seed in March and April 13mm deep in a seedbed, with 25-30cm in and between the rows. Thin to leave the strongest seedling. Or, sow seeds in 7.5cm pots of good compost.

Transplant to their permanent position when they are large enough to handle, allowing 60-90cm between plants, and water and feed.

Seed-grown plants flower the year of sowing. Remove flower heads. They crop best in year two and three. Cut and trim heads to eat.

Jerusalem artichokes are root vegetables that grow from tubers planted in March and April at 10-15cm deep and 30cm apart. They grow up to more than 2m tall. Prune to 8cm in winter. The cut stakes are useful to hold plants up. Harvest the roots to use as root vegetables.

Jerusalem artichokes at the edge

sterile demijohns with an airlock. Leave it to ferment for two weeks. Siphon and then leave to ferment for another fortnight. Siphon into sealed sterile bottles and store for a few weeks to mature.

Pears, pear juice and perry cider all follow similar ideas. When growing pears, peaches, cherries and other top fruit, follow the same principles as apple tree growing.

COOK

To dry, use clean, dry, pitted, sliced fruit and place on a baking tray in the oven at 175F for 10-12 hours. Turn them halfway.

Clean, core and slice the apples, then soak in a lemon juice solution for 10 minutes to stop browning, then place in the oven as for apricots. Add spices beforehand such as cinnamon. Try drying in the sun for a couple of days

on a tray, or in a dehydrator.

Add to muesli/granola as a fruity improver.

ARTICHOKES

(Globe/Jerusalem)

Jerusalem artichokes are one of those magic crops that appear year after year and add height, drama, and crop a useful root veg too. Globe artichokes are basically edible thistles and add a meaty component to any plate.

NUTRITION

Globe per 100g:
- Folates 68µg (one millionth of a gram) 17% Recommended Daily Allowance (RDA)

Globe artichokes, which are high in copper, folates and iron. Jerusalem artichokes are a root crop.

EAT

of a plot act as a windbreak. Along with a beetle bank, hedge and wild area. They are best known for causing flatulence. The storage carbohydrate is inulin instead of starch, which breaks down into fructose sugars so is a low-calorific food and is useful in diabetic diets. Inulin is included in probiotic drinks that contain cultures of good bacteria but it is not broken down in the gut so causes flatulence.

Grilled Jerusalem artichokes with heritage carrots:

Ingredients
1kg artichokes
80ml olive oil
150ml white wine vinegar
600g carrots
300g pea shoots

Method
Cook peeled and sliced artichokes for 1 hour, peel and slice
Griddle with oil
Marinate with vinegar
Soak carrots in vinegar and make salad

ASPARAGUS

Asparagus are classic British perennials that used to be as expensive and rare as caviar, but are now more widely available fresh – and as a perennial are worthwhile to grow.

NUTRITION

· Folates	52 µg	13%
· Riboflavin	0.141 mg	11%
· Thiamin	0.143 mg	12%
· Vitamin C	5.6 mg	9%
· Vitamin A	756 IU (international unit)	25%
· Vitamin E	1.13 mg	7.5%
· Vitamin K	41.6 µg	35%
· Copper	0.189 mg	21%
· Iron	1.14 mg	14%

GROW

Plant crowns (roots-which you buy) in early spring or autumn and leave for at least a year to store up some energy. Let the fern develop and only cut it down when yellow in late autumn. Asparagus spears should be cut when they reach around 15cm tall. Cut spears individually at about 2cm below ground level. Only cut a few in year two or it weakens the plant.

Asparagus contains high levels of the amino acid asparagine, making it a natural diuretic, flushing excess fluid and salt from the body, which may help prevent urinary tract infections.

Asparagus were once known as a posh veg, rarely available, that you wrapped in ham or soggy white sliced bread, and which made your urine smell. Worse still were flaccid spears tinned in brine, to be dipped in rubbery Hollandaise.

EAT

To eat asparagus, make the most of its freshness. Snap shoots off in the garden and boil or fry very lightly. I'd dip it in hummus, eat it in risotto, skewer five together to barbecue and dip in soy sauce, or serve in a vegan tempura batter. Boil or fry lightly and then use in pasta or risotto dishes, or as a side. Asparagus is expensive so do not waste the woody ends. Blend them to add flavour to a soya milk sauce for pasta. But whatever modern way you serve asparagus, the urine thing is still the same.

AUBERGINE

Another 'posh' veg, difficult to grow but a real achievement if you do. This big purple sack of a vegetable is one of the best to show off, if you get it right.

NUTRITION

· Dietary Fibre	3.40 g	9%
· Potassium	230 mg	5%
· Copper	0.082 mg	9%
· Manganese	0.250 mg	11%

GROW

Aubergines are tricky to grow because they need a lot of warmth. Sow at 18-21°C in seed-sowing compost in pots or modules. If you are sowing for a windowsill, sow from late February. For outdoor growing, sow inside in early March, and hope for a warm summer. Plant out at the end of May in soil you have covered to warm it up. Plant in a sunny spot. You can buy young plants in garden centres, which are often grafted. Grow in 9cm pots initially, and then transfer plants to 23cm pots in April in a heated greenhouse, which is the preferable environment for this crop. Water

regularly and feed with a high potassium liquid fertiliser every two weeks once the first fruit has set. Mist the foliage with a sprayer twice daily with luke-warm water to discourage red spider mite and help fruit set.

EAT

Aubergine is a meaty vegetable so use as you would meat in a curry or chilli.

A classic aubergine dish is Aubergine Parmigiana:

Ingredients
Two aubergines
400g tomatoes
50g vegan cheese
Pinch vegan Parmesan

Method
Heat oven to 200C. Put the aubergines on a baking tray and slit down the centre of each. Drizzle with 2 tbsp olive oil and season. Bake for 50-55 mins or until the flesh is soft. Heat the grill. Tip a 400g can of tomatoes into a bowl and season. Fill the aubergines with layers of tomatoes and vegan mozzarella, and finish with vegan Parmesan. Put under the grill for 5-7 mins.

BEETROOT

A real superfood that has moved on from being a school dinner horror into being a fresh delight.

NUTRITION

· Folates	109 µg	27%
· Vitamin C	4.9 mg	8%
· Potassium	325 mg	7%
· Copper	0.075 mg	8%
· Iron	0.80 mg	10%
· Magnesium	23 mg	6%
· Manganese	0.329 mg	14%

GROW

Sow seeds directly into the soil from mid-spring. Like all roots, beetroot just grows. Watch for bolting or leaving too long so the beetroot goes woody. That means tender golf ball, or slightly more mature cricket balled sized.

EAT

Beetroot always used to be pickled in vinegar, leaking red onto your school shirt cuffs, from whence it would never come off. Instead of eating the vinegary, eye-watering pickles, juice, boil, use in dips, soups, risottos, eat raw in salads or use in sweet cakes.

BORSCHT
Ingredients
300g beetroot
Onion
Carrot
Leek
2 sticks celery
Half cabbage
Four cloves of garlic
2 vegetable stock cubes
2 tsp oil
Vegan feta (optional)

Method
Peel and slice vegetables then soften the root vegetables in a deep pan with the oil. Add the beetroot after 10 minutes then add the stock and garlic and simmer for 40 minutes. Blitz until smooth then add vegan feta to taste.

BLUEBERRIES

A fruit that was barely available a couple of decades ago but is now commonplace and is relatively easy to grow yourself.

NUTRITION

· Carbohydrates	14.49 g	11%
· Vitamin C	9.7 mg	15%
· Vitamin K	19.3 µg	13%
· Manganese	0.336 mg	14%

GROW

Grow in acidic (5.5pH lime-free) soil in a large container. Use ericaceous fertiliser and rainwater. Net from birds. Oak leaves, pine needles or coffee grounds can add acidity. Good for heart, eyes and memory.

EAT

Eat raw or as an ingredient in a pancake or cheesecake.

CHEESECAKE
Ingredients
200g dates
120g walnuts
180g cashews
Lemon
80g coconut oil
150ml coconut milk
120ml syrup
A few blueberries

Method
Blend the dates and walnuts. Pack into a greased muffin tin (or line the tin with parchment).

Blend the cashews, juice of a lemon, coconut oil, coconut milk and agave nectar or maple syrup.
Divide filling evenly among the muffin tins. Drop in blueberries (or other fruits). Freeze for 4-6 hours.

PANCAKE
Ingredients
175g plain flour
2tbsp chickpea flour
1tsp baking powder
175ml soya milk
1 tbsp vegetable oil
A few blueberries

Method
Mix the plain flour, chickpea flour and baking powder together with the soya milk, 175ml of water and 1 tbsp vegetable oil. Add a few blueberries. Heat the oil in a frying pan and add enough mix to cover the bottom. Fry for one minute, loosen the edges with a spatula and flip, then fry the other side.

BROAD BEANS

(Fava)

Beans are great for iron, protein, and soluble fibre to decrease bad cholesterol and contain potassium, calcium, vitamins B, and zinc. Broad beans growing up a wigwam don't take up much space and add a bit of structure to the garden.

NUTRITION

· Energy	341 Kcal	15%
· Carbohydrates	58.59 g	45%
· Protein	26.12 g	46.5%
· Dietary Fibre	25 g	66%
· Folates	423 µg	106%
· Niacin	2.832 mg	18%
· Pantothenic acid	0.976 mg	19.5%
· Pyridoxine	0.366 mg	28%
· Riboflavin	0.333 mg	25%
· Thiamin	0.555 mg	46.25%
· Vitamin K	9 µg	7.5%
· Potassium	1062 mg	23%
· Calcium	103 mg	10%
· Copper	0.824 µg	91%
· Iron	6.70 mg	84%
· Magnesium	192 mg	18%
· Manganese	1.626 mg	71%
· Phosphorus	421 mg	60%
· Selenium	8.2 µg	15%
· Zinc	3.14 mg	9%

GROW

Sow beans in autumn for an early crop in spring, or in spring for a later crop. Young plants can go in during May. Plant beans 5cm deep and 20cm apart. They should take 10 days to germinate and may need staking as they grow taller.

EAT

Remove from pods. Eat raw with skins removed (eating raw is dangerous if you have a G6P deficiency). Purée and serve with fried garlic. Boil broad beans as a side and serve with mint leaves.

BROAD BEAN HUMMUS
Ingredients
450g broad beans
100g tinned chickpeas
2 tbsp tahini
I tbsp lemon juice

Method
Cook the broad beans in boiling water for two minutes then remove the green inner skins when cool.
Blitz all the ingredients in a food processor, adding the water from the tin of chickpeas.
Season to taste.

BRUSSEL SPROUTS

Another school dinner joke veg. But sprouts are more than that; as a winter veg, they are useful to fill a seasonal gap on the plot, and nutritionally, sprouts provide a rich range of benefits.

NUTRITION

· Carbohydrates	8.95 g	7%
· Protein	3.38 g	6%
· Dietary Fibre	3.80 g	10%
· Folates	61 µg	15%
· Pyridoxine	0.219 mg	17%
· Thiamin	0.139 mg	13%
· Vitamin A	754 IU	25%
· Vitamin C	85 mg	142%
· Vitamin K	177 µg	147%
· Potassium	389 mg	8%
· Copper	0.70 mg	8%
· Iron	1.40 mg	17.5%
· Magnesium	23 mg	6%

Image/Terry Pixabay

BROCCOLI

A vegetable that goes in and out of fashion, usurping the cauliflower, then losing out to trendy kale. Whatever, broccoli is one of the best to grow and eat.

NUTRITION

· Carbohydrates	6.64 g	5%
· Protein	2.82 g	5%
· Dietary Fibre	2.60 g	7%
· Folates	63 µg	16%
· Pantothenic acid	0.573 mg	12%
· Pyridoxine	0.175 mg	13%
· Riboflavin	0.117 mg	9%
· Thiamin	0.071 mg	6%
· Vitamin A	623 IU	21%
· Vitamin C	89.2 mg	149%
· Vitamin K	101.6 µg	85%
· Potassium	316 mg	7%
· Calcium	47 mg	5%
· Copper	0.049 mg	5.5%
· Iron	0.73 mg	9%
· Magnesium	21 mg	5%
· Manganese	0.210 mg	9%
· Selenium	2.5 µg	5%
· Zinc	0.41 mg	4%

GROW

Sow seeds between March and June, in a greenhouse or indoors until April and outside from April. Add liquid fertiliser every week and plant out in well manured soil when 10-15cm high.

Allow 30cm between plants and 45cm between rows. You can plant direct outside from April 2cm deep, covered with fleece to try and ward off root fly and slugs and snails. Water and fertilise. Net from birds.

EAT

Add to pasta or salad such as quinoa, squash and broccoli salad. Serve as a side such as broccoli and green beans boiled then tossed in fried nut butter.

| · Manganese | 0.337 mg | 15% |
| · Phosphorus | 69 mg | 10% |

GROW

Sprout seeds are best sown in spring in pots or trays under glass or in a seedbed, protected by a cloche. Treat like other brassicas such as cabbage and kale and transplant to their final positions when 15cm high in May-June. Plant out 60cm-75cm apart.

EAT

Sprouts are very good for you but have a bad reputation as an over-boiled Christmas food, recently made worse by celebrity chefs invariably 'livening them up' by cooking them with bacon. Try miso roasted sprouts. In a roasting tin, toss Brussel sprouts with miso paste melted in olive oil. Roast for 15-20 minutes.

CABBAGE

As unfashionable as they come, until people realised it has high vitamin C and K and doesn't need to be boiled for hours.

NUTRITION

· Carbohydrates	5.8 g	4%
· Dietary Fibre	2.50 mg	6%
· Folates	53 µg	13%
· Vitamin C	36.6 mg	61%
· Vitamin K	76 µg	63%
· Iron	0.47 mg	6%
· Manganese	0.160 mg	7%

GROW

Use the same method as broccoli and other brassicas. Net well to stop bird and caterpillar nibblers.

EAT

COLCANNON:
Ingredients
Five potatoes
One cabbage
Three leeks
100ml soya milk

Method
Boil the potatoes until tender. In a separate pan, steam the chopped cabbage for five minutes. Cook three sliced leeks in soya milk for 15 minutes. Mash potatoes and leeks, add cabbage and stir to combine. Season.

CARROTS

An orange vegetable like a carrot has special qualities you can infer without knowing anything about nutritional science. The power of vitamin A is anti-ageing, anti-cancer and good for the skin. The beat-carotene, denoted by the orange, converts into vitamin A in the liver, and is actually good for the retina. Carrots contain falcarinol, a natural compound that may stimulate cancer-fighting mechanisms in the body. Carrots are a valuable source of antioxidants, which may help to ward off damage from free radicals, slowing down cellular aging. Calcium in carrots helps prevent the narrowing of the blood vessels resulting from contracting of the muscular wall of the vessels. Potassium promotes regular heartbeat. Vitamin B improves metabolism. Vitamin C protects cells against free radicals and strengthens blood vessel walls. Vitamin A in carrot is important in vision; a deficiency in vitamin A will inhibit the reformation of rhodopsin and lead to night blindness.

(Klimkin Pixabay)

NUTRITION

· Carbohydrates	9.58 g	7%
· Dietary Fibre	2.8 g	7%
· Folates	19 µg	5%
· Niacin	0.983 mg	6%
· Pantothenic acid	0.273 mg	5.5%
· Pyridoxine	0.138 mg	10%
· Thiamin	0.066 mg	6%
· Vitamin A	16706 IU	557%
· Vitamin C	5.9 mg	10%
· Vitamin K	13.2 µg	11%
· Potassium	320 mg	6.5%
· Manganese	0.143 mg	6%
· Phosphorus	35 mg	5%

GROW

Carrots are more difficult to grow than most roots because of carrot fly. Sow seeds thinly where the carrots are to grow. Stony, clay soil inhibits root growth. Sandy soil is best. If you thin out seedlings, carrot fly will smell them and attack, making holes in the roots. Netting is the only way to put off the fly. After planting, let them grow, for three or four months. Carrots are associated with a 32% lower risk of coronary heart disease.

EAT

Use in juicing, cakes, salads, soup, as a side.

CARROT CAKE:
Ingredients
250ml oil
300g sugar
200ml soya milk
400g plain flour
1.5 tsp baking powder
1.5tsp bicarbonate of soda
Spices
300g grated carrots.

Method
Heat the oven to 180C/160C fan/gas mark 4. Grease 2 x 20cm cake tins with oil and line the bases with baking parchment. Whisk together the oil and sugar. Add the milk. Mix the flour, baking powder, bicarbonate of soda and spices in a separate dish. Add the mixtures together and stir, then stick in the carrot. Spoon into the tins and bake for 25-30 mins.

CAULIFLOWER

Always my favourite vegetable, and now new coloured varieties make the 'humble' cauli a more attractive proposition than the over boiled mushy grey florets many remember.

NUTRITION

· Folates	57 µg	14%
· Pantothenic acid	0.667 mg	13%
· Pyridoxine	0.184 mg	14%
· Vitamin C	48.2 mg	80%
· Vitamin K	15.5 µg	13%
· Potassium	299 mg	6%
· Iron	0.42 mg	5%
· Manganese	0.155 mg	7%

GROW

Grow in a similar way to broccoli or cabbage.

EAT

CAULIFLOWER CHEESE:
Macaroni cheese has become a fashionable dish but lacks many nutrients and is high in fat. Cauliflower cheese is better.

Ingredients
One cauliflower
One leek
50g plain flour
400ml soya milk
200g vegan cheese
½ tsp mustard
1 tsp Marmite
40g yeast flakes

Method
Fry a leek then add the flour and cook for one minute while stirring. Add the soya milk and 400ml of water a bit at a time, stirring throughout. Slowly bring to the boil. Whisk out any lumps. Add the mustard, Marmite, vegan cheese, yeast flakes and season. Meanwhile steam or boil a cauliflower and serve with the sauce on top.

CELERY

Like so many vegetables, celery is ruined by cooking. Raw food is often best as cooking can lose nutrients, texture and taste.

NUTRITION

· Carbohydrates	3 g	5.5%
· Protein	3.46 g	6%
· Dietary Fibre	2.10 g	5.5%
· Folates	36 µg	9%
· Pantothenic acid	0.246 mg	5%
· Pyridoxine	0.074 mg	6%
· Vitamin A	449 IU	15%
· Vitamin C	3.1 mg	5%
· Vitamin K	29.3 µg	24%
· Sodium	80 mg	5%
· Potassium	260 mg	5.5%

GROW

Celery is difficult to grow from seed because the seeds are small and may need a propagator to germinate. You can buy seedlings to plant when frosts have passed about 27cm apart in a grid pattern making sure the crown of the plant is at ground level. Water, fertilise and weed. Harvest from August.

EAT

My opinion is to never cook celery. It turns to stringy mush. Wash well and use in salads and as a dipper in hummus.

COURGETTE

(Zucchini)

One of the most satisfying crops to grow, as the fruits appear as if from nowhere, while the early flowers and later marrows are edible too. Courgettes are particularly good for heart-healthy potassium.

NUTRITION

· Folates	24 µg	6%
· Pantothenic acid	0.204 mg	5%
· Pyridoxine	0.163 mg	13%
· Riboflavin	0.094 mg	7%
· Vitamin A	200 IU	7%
· Vitamin C	17.9 mg	30%
· Potassium	261 mg	5.5%
· Manganese	0.177 mg	8%
· Phosphorus	38 mg	5%

GROW

Start indoors in pots sowing from March-May singly 1.5cm deep. Keep at 15-20 degrees C. Plant out May-June. The knack is to get them going, then get them going again outside. They are slug bait, so need protection, which should be a barrier such as grit around the young plants, not a slug killer. Feed with lots of comfrey fertiliser and water regularly.

Catch them before they bolt into marrows. Unless you want a watery old zeppelin to try and find a recipe for.

EAT

Courgettes can either be steamed, stir-fried, baked, microwaved, stuffed and roasted. They can also be eaten raw.

(Steveph Pi.

Marrow wine

One of the most expensive items in the household budget is booze. That's because of the tax you have to pay. But levy-free alcohol can be crafted out of returning to your plot after a week away on holiday (or just being lazy) to find about three tonnes of marrows growing. And there were only a couple of courgettes when you left... This could be your answer when sceptics ask 'Why do people bother growing their own – haven't they heard of shops?'

To sort the marrow problem and make some wine to serve to your (hopefully impressed) friends, ferment the monsters with sugar and a packet of wine yeast (about £1 mail-order from

any home-brew shop). Put in enough sugar to get it to 4%: shouldn't take more than two weeks. Add some 'wine nutrient' to avoid headache wine. Do it in the bath or get a seven gallon beer or plastic wine fermenter: only about £10. Don't use non-food grade plastic buckets as the colouring can be toxic and gets leached in to the booze.

Alternatively (or as well), homemade vodka is one of the most popular alcoholic beverages. It is a colourless liquid that consists mostly of distilled water and ethanol. Both water and ethanol are purified through several processes of distillation. You need 2.2 lbs. of potatoes per litre. Peel and chop and cook (ideally in a pressure cooker) until dissolved. Strain to extract the potato juice. Now you need a distilling kit (online or at beer- and wine-making shops) to remove impurities from your extracted potato juice, giving you a pure potato vodka.

Try the hooch or wine on your muesli (preferably homemade). Nutritious and gets you drunk. It's called buesli.

Three alternative ideas

· You can use courgette/marrows in ratatouille. Lightly sauté garlic in olive oil, add diced onions, aubergines, peppers, tomatoes and herbs. Stew it all up together for an hour or more.

· Another way to use up big marrows is to peel, seed and dice finely. Place in a big bowl, with finely chopped garlic, salt, pepper and olive oil. Mix well, turn out into a big shallow gratin dish. Bung into medium oven for a couple of hours. Top with vegan cheese towards the end of the cooking time.

· Grate marrow coarsely and wring out in a kitchen cloth to get rid of the juice, soften spring onions with garlic in a pan, add grated marrow. Stir in some flour and vegan egg to bind, break in vegan cheese and dill. Shape into patties and fry carefully. Suitable for freezing.

CURRANTS

(Black - Red - White)

Ribena, only available when you were ill (for the vitamin C) or at birthday parties (as a sugary treat), used to be the best way to taste a blackcurrant. Now you can find varieties sweet enough to eat. Blander blueberries have usurped the blackcurrant, but currants have more complex flavours, well worth cultivating.

NUTRITION

· Carbohydrates	15.38 g	12%
· Dietary Fibre	4.3 g	11%
· Pantothenic acid	0.398 mg	8%
· Vitamin A	230 IU	7.5%
· Vitamin C	181 mg	301%
· Potassium	322 mg	7%
· Calcium	55 mg	5.5%
· Copper	0.086 mg	9.5%
· Iron	1.54 mg	19.5%
· Magnesium	24 mg	6%
· Manganese	0.256 mg	11%
· Phosphorus	59 mg	8.5%

GROW

Bare-root plants should be planted from late autumn; containerised plants can be planted at any time of year. Cover with netting as the fruits develop. Prune blackcurrants when dormant – from late autumn to late winter. Fruit forms on young wood, so when pruning aim to remove older wood, leaving the young shoots. Also, grow in pots.

EAT

Jam, juice or include in many puddings.

EDAMAME/ SOYA BEAN

This is magic food that when left to mature can be made into soya milk or tofu soya 'meat', which has become the staple of many vegetarian and vegan diets. You can attempt to make milk yourself from mature beans or harvest when young and use like a broad bean or pea.

NUTRITION

· Energy	109 Kcal	5.5%
· Carbohydrates	7.61 g	6%
· Protein	11.22 g	20%
· Total Fat	4.73 g	23.5%
· Dietary Fibre	4.8 g	13%
· Folates	303 µg	76%
· Pantothenic acid	0.535 mg	11%
· Pyridoxine	0.135 mg	10%
· Riboflavin	0.265 mg	20%
· Thiamin	0.150 mg	12.5%
· Vitamin C	9.7 mg	16%
· Vitamin K	31.4 µg	26%
· Potassium	482 mg	10%
· Copper	0.324 µg	36%
· Iron	2.11 mg	26%
· Magnesium	224 mg	56%
· Manganese	1.672 mg	73%
· Phosphorus	161 mg	23%
· Zinc	1.32 µg	12%

GROW

Sow in May and early June 5cm deep in 7.5cm pots or trays of seed compost. Put in a propagator, or seal inside a polythene bag, and heat to 18-20°C.

The seeds won't germinate outside until the soil is warm enough, at least 15 degrees. Plant 15cm apart in rows 45cm apart. Plant seeds 2.5cm deep, spacing them 10cm apart in rows. Cover with soil and water well. Keep the soil moist until the seeds germinate.

After germinating inside, grow plants on by placing on a windowsill. Move seedlings into larger pots when roots appear through the drainage holes in the base and gradually acclimatise to outdoor conditions before planting out after frosts.

Plants grow over 1m high but support themselves. Water and mulch. When the beans are almost touching one another inside the pod, and the raw beans taste mild and sweet, the edamame is ready to harvest.

Soya is a legume, like a pea. Grows in pods. Like a pea. They can also be sown directly outside once the soil has warmed up in late spring. Don't plant seedlings until soil is above 55° F.

EAT

Boil cooked pods or beans as a side dish, tossed in soy sauce and sesame

seeds. To make a dip, cook and mix in a food processor. Add water if necessary. Mix in lime juice, salt, Tabasco and sesame oil to taste. Soya also produces tofu/bean curd set soya milk and is fermented as tempeh or miso or soya sauce.

FENNEL

A salad vegetable that is unusual in that it gains flavour when cooked, when the aniseed taste becomes richer and more subtle.

NUTRITION

Dietary Fibre	3.1 g	8%
Folates	27 µg	7%
Pantothenic acid	0.232 mg	5%
Vitamin C	12 mg	20%
Potassium	414 mg	9%
Calcium	49 mg	5%
Copper	0.066 mg	7%

| Iron | 0.73 mg | 9% |
| Phosphorus | 50 mg | 9% |

GROW

Sow outdoors thinly and cover with 1.5cm of soil. Seedlings appear in 7-21 days. Thin to 20cm apart. Earth up bulbs and water. Harvest July-October when 10cm across.

EAT

Use leaves and sliced for salads or roast bulbs for an aniseed-flavoured veg. Eat raw in salads with citrus or cook the aniseedy base and stems of fennel by braising or roasting, which make it sweet and tender. Cut off the root end and the leaves and peel the outer layer of skin away, next cut either downwards or across the bulb, then boil in salted water for about 15 minutes, or until tender. Fennel is good for making soup or it can be poached, steamed or boiled.

Roast fennel.

GOOSEBERRIES

Gooseberries are another crop with negative connotations that nutritional science has managed to turn around. Full of vitamin C, and growing is genuinely easy.

NUTRITION

· Carbohydrates	10.18 g	8%
· Dietary Fibre	4.3 g	11%
· Pantothenic acid	0.286 mg	6%
· Vitamin A	290 IU	10%
· Vitamin C	27.7 mg	46%
· Copper	0.070 mg	8%

GROW

Plant bare-root gooseberries between late autumn and early spring, and container-grown plants at any time. Give plenty of space-they spread and are

hard to prune because of the thorns. Make sure there is no bindweed where you plant them because this will be difficult to remove once the bush is established. Cover with a net when fruits start to develop to deter birds.

EAT

Green, under-ripe fruits are good for jam, pies, tarts, and sauces in June. Pick riper, sweeter fruit in July.

Ingredients
200g gooseberries
100g sugar
250ml vegan whipping cream
Vanilla pod
50g icing sugar

Method
For gooseberry fool, put gooseberries and sugar in a pan with a splash of water. Heat gently, stirring, then bring to a simmer and cook until the fruit starts to burst. Mash the gooseberries, then chill. Whisk vegan whipping cream in a bowl with icing sugar and vanilla until smooth. Add the gooseberry pulp.

HAZELNUTS/ FILBERTS/ COBNUTS

(Miriams-fotos P)

Nuts make a big difference to a diet where you may not be eating meat or dairy. They have an astonishing wide variety of nutrients and are full of energy with 100g containing 628 Kcal.

Walnuts, hazels and sweet chestnuts are growable. Hazels include cobnuts and filberts. Nut trees provide décor, shade, attract wildlife and pest predators and shed leaves for mulch and leaf mould.

NUTRITION

· Energy	628 Kcal	31%
· Carbohydrates	16.7 g	13%
· Protein	14.95g	26.5%
· Total Fat	60.75 g	202%
· Cholesterol	0 mg	0%
· Dietary Fibre	9.7 g	25.5%
· Folates	113 µg	28%
· Niacin	1.8 mg	11%
· Pantothenic acid	0.918 mg	18%
· Pyridoxine	0.563 mg	43%
· Riboflavin	0.113 mg	9%
· Thiamin	0.643 mg	53.5%
· Vitamin C	6.3 mg	10.5%
· Vitamin E	15 mg	100%
· Vitamin K	14.2 µg	12%
· Potassium	680 mg	14%
· Calcium	114 mg	11%
· Copper	1.725 mg	192%
· Iron	4.7 mg	59%
· Magnesium	163 mg	41%
· Manganese	6.17 mg	268%
· Phosphorus	290 mg	41%
· Zinc	2.45 mg	22%

GROW

Plant two different varieties, which are known to pollinate each other. If you have wild hazel bushes nearby, they will also act as a pollinator; wind pollinates hazels within a 50m range. Male catkins and red-tipped female flowers appear on the same tree but at different times, so trees are self-sterile. It is best to buy trees that are two years old. Planting nuts will produce weak plants.

In autumn, plant bare root young trees bought from the garden centre or nursery. Dig a hole one and a half times the size of the root ball. Support walnuts and chestnuts with a tree stake. Mulch to keep in moisture and keep weeds down. Prune away suckers and shape the tree in late summer

You can propagate new trees by cutting off rooted suckers and planting them in pots. Ideally, plant in square groups in winter when the trees are dormant. Feed, mulch and, in summer, water. Protect with wire netting from rodents and rabbits. 'Cosford' is a good cobnut variety choice. Cobnuts and filberts should start to produce nuts after three or four years. They should be harvested when the husks begin to turn yellow around late September. Get them before fully ripe, ahead of the squirrels.

EAT

Open with a nut cracker. Store opened nuts in an airtight container for up to three months. Eat raw or added to muesli. Chop and use in cakes or crumble toppings. Grind to make flour for baking.

Other nuts:
Sweet or Spanish chestnuts are common and can be eaten fresh and raw when removed from their hedgehog-like shells or, more traditionally, roasted. Sweet chestnuts need acidic soil and they spread, so need plenty of space. The horse chestnut or conker is inedible.

Walnuts are growable. Freshly fallen walnuts are known as 'wet' nuts. They don't keep well. You can pickle the green ones. Commercial nuts are artificially dried and will keep longer. Almonds need lots of sun to fruit so flourish when trained as a fan on a south-facing wall with fleece as protection in winter.

HERBS

A massive area of horticulture, though you don't need a massive area to grow them. Herbs can go in just about any food or drink and they can all be grown at home, indoor or out.

Many herbs prefer sun and dry, fairly thin soil – Mediterranean-style conditions. In pots, add grit to the compost for drainage.

Consider basil, chives (perennial), mint (an invasive perennial so plant in a pot), parsley, rosemary (a shrub), sage (a shrub), savoury, tarragon, thyme (shrub), lavender, coriander, chervil, borage and fennel.

Herbs can also work well mixed in with other plants, and are beneficial neighbours in some cases. Fast growers such as parsley, coriander, dill and chervil work well in gaps in the veg patch.

Borage is helpful among strawberries in attracting pollinators. Borage flowers are said to drive out melancholy. Who would not benefit from this? Bees love them too, and watching bees buzzing for a while can take away the blues too. In spring, direct seed the herb, which is a good companion plant for tomatoes, squash and strawberries.

You can also grow herbs indoors hydroponically using a pre-mixed nutrient solution provided to plants that are grown without soil often under lights. You will need to buy a system.

Map out where you plan to plant your herb plants, thinking about how big they will become when designing spacing. A sunny spot works best. Pots, hanging baskets or raised beds with grit dug in may work better for rosemary, lavender and thyme, which suffer when their roots get wet. Or mix them between other plants, where they work well as aphid attracters. There are annuals

such as basil, coriander, and marjoram; perennials such as mint, fennel and thyme and bushy perennials such as rosemary, lavender, thyme and sage.

GROW

Sow seeds direct outside from March until August.

Or sow under cover in seed trays or modules and plant them out later.

Basil fares best indoors on a sunny windowsill.

Plant perennial seeds such as rosemary, sage, chives and fennel under cover.

Sow seeds of perennial herbs such as rosemary, sage, chives and fennel in the spring under cover in a warm place. Then pot them on when large enough to handle. Harden off plants in a cold frame before planting out into their final positions. Otherwise, buy ready-grown plants.

Lots of herbs are difficult to start off. Parsley is a struggle as are basil and tarragon. You're better off buying a supermarket plant and keeping it on your windowsill. Divide the plant and plant separately into the ground.

Herbs you can grow straight from seed planted onto your patch include: wild rocket, which is great as peppery salad leaves, borage to attract bees (not much use for eating) and coriander as a curry garnish.

Sow chervil and dill direct from March-August because they are difficult to transplant. Mint spreads fast so grow in sunken buckets or plastic pots with holes in restrict root growth. The woodier plants such as rosemary, thyme and sage are better planted as young plug plants, rather than messing about with seeds.

KALE

Justifiably a vegetable de jour, kale is a nutritional powerhouse. It grows in winter and tastes ok, if you can cook out the bitterness.

NUTRITION

· Carbohydrates	8.75 g	7%
· Protein	4.28 g	8%
· Dietary Fibre	3.6 g	9%
· Folates	141 µg	35%
· Pyridoxine	0.271 mg	21%
· Riboflavin	0.130 mg	10%
· Thiamin	0.110 mg	9%
· Vitamin A	9990 IU	333%
· Vitamin C	120 mg	200%
· Vitamin K	704.8 µg	587%
· Potassium	491 mg	10.5%
· Calcium	150 mg	15%
· Copper	1.499 mg	166%
· Iron	1.47 mg	18%
· Magnesium	47mg	12%
· Manganese	0.659 mg	28%
· Phosphorus	92 mg	12%

GROW

Sow outdoors thinly from April-June in prepared seed bed and cover with 1.5cm soil. Transplant to final position 45cm apart. Cut at 7.5cm tall and they will regrow for several cuts. Harvest in winter-frosts enhance flavour.

EAT

Break the leaves from the stalk, and trim away the tough centre stalk. Wash, then shred or chop, then boil. Kale is great in stir fries, added to soups, crisped in the oven in a tray with a little oil and salt, blitzed in a smoothie, or braised, fried, baked, steamed, blanched, sautéed or tossed in a salad.

KOHL RABI

Looks and tastes a bit exotic. A crisp and light, mild, knobbly, bulbous, juicy brassica that looks like an alien's head; it should be more widely grown and eaten.

NUTRITION

· Carbohydrates	6.20 g	5%
· Dietary Fibre	3.6 g	10%
· Vitamin C	62 mg	102%
· Potassium	350 mg	7%
· Copper	0.129 mg	14%
· Iron	0.40 mg	5%
· Magnesium	19 mg	5%
· Manganese	0.139 mg	6%
· Phosphorus	46 mg	6.5%

GROW

Sow outdoors March-July in prepared soil 1.5cm deep. Seedlings appear in 7-21 days. Thin to 15cm apart.

Use raw in salads or boiled. Puree kohl rabi into soups or eat as fritters when dipped in a vegan batter and deep fried. Roasted, kohl rabi caramelises and sweetens and forms a good partnership with other root vegetables.

LEEKS

A really versatile and under-appreciated vegetable that is not that hard to grow. Adds flavour and bulk to dishes and has many nutritional benefits.

NUTRITION

· Carbohydrates	14.15 g	11%
· Dietary Fibre	1.8 g	5%
· Folates	64 μg	16%
· Pyridoxine	0.233 mg	18%
· Vitamin A	1667 IU	55%
· Vitamin C	12 mg	20%
· Vitamin E	0.92 mg	6%
· Vitamin K	47 μg	39%
· Calcium	59 mg	6 %
· Copper	0.120 mg	13%
· Iron	2.10 mg	26%
· Magnesium	28 mg	7%
· Zinc	1.2 mg	11%

GROW

Grow leeks by sowing seed directly into the soil in rows 30cm apart and 1cm deep in a trench that you cover over between March and April. Or buy ready-grown seedlings and plant out from May in a 20cm hole with the seedling watered in. Being underground blanches the stems white. When seedlings have three leaves each, thin to leave plants every 15cm. Weed, mulch and water. You can pick from summer or leave until later in the year.

EAT

Roast with other vegetables in olive oil with herbs. Add to mashed potatoes. Leek and potato soup is a classic.

Ingredients
400g leeks
500g potatoes
1 vegetable stock cube

Method
Wash leeks and potatoes and peel the potatoes. Chop them into bite size pieces. Fry the leeks. Dissolve a vegetable stock cube in 1.2 litres of water. Put the chopped vegetables into a large pan with the stock and bring to boil. Season.

LETTUCE

After the potato, just about the easiest crop to grow, inside or out. Experiment with dressings to liven the many different types of lettuce up. Rocket is one of the best for flavour.

NUTRITION

· Folates	38 μg	9.5%
· Pyridoxine	0.090 mg	7%
· Riboflavin	0.080 mg	6 %
· Thiamin	0.070 mg	6%
· Vitamin A	7405 IU	247%
· Vitamin C	9.2 mg	15%
· Vitamin K	126.3 μg	105%
· Iron	0.86 mg	10%
· Manganese	0.250 mg	11%
· Phosphorus	29g	4%

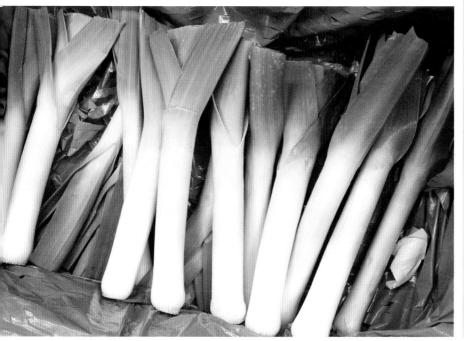

GROW

Sow seed outdoors from late March to late July. Plant seedlings as soon as the first true leaves appear 30cm (12in) apart. If you sow later, plants may need to be protected under cloches in autumn. Otherwise, you can grow lettuce on a windowsill indoors. Pick outer leaves and the inside will keep growing.

EAT

Eat in salads, obviously. But you can cook lettuce. Grill a half head and use as a side, or add to a soup for a bit of crunch. Add freshness, texture and colour to wraps and rolls.

Salad dressing ideas: 3 tbsp vegan mayo, whisked with lemon juice with herbs added.

· Olive oil/balsamic vinegar/herbs. Tahini, maple syrup, lemon juice or cider vinegar, vegetable oil. Add cayenne or curry powder for a curry dressing.

· Avocado, oil, lemon, parsley, garlic, seasoning-blended.

· French/wholegrain mustard, maple syrup, vegan mayo, orange juice. Peanut butter, soya sauce, maple/agave syrup.

ONIONS/GARLIC

Cheap to buy, easy to grow, and ubiquitous in almost all recipes. Try more interesting varieties.

NUTRITION

· Carbohydrates	9.34 g	7%
· Dietary Fibre	1.7 g	4.5%
· Folates	19 µg	5%
· Pyridoxine	0.120 mg	9%
· Vitamin C	7.4 mg	12%
· Manganese	0.129 mg	5.5%
· Phosphorus	29 mg	4%

GROW

You can grow onions and shallots either from seed or from onion sets (small bulbs). Seeds take longer. Onion and shallot sets are available for spring planting for harvesting that year or autumn planting, to be harvested the next year.

Plant shallot and onion sets so that the tip of bulb is sticking through the soil surface. Leave a space of 10cm between each bulb, and 30cm between each row.

Sow seed direct outdoors in spring as the soil begins to warm up. Sow thinly 1cm deep and with 30cm between rows. Thin onion seedlings to 10cm apart for medium sized bulbs.

Or start in the greenhouse or on a windowsill in module trays. Place the trays in a propagator or seal them inside a plastic bag at a temperature of 10-15C until after germination. Once germinated, grow on until after the frosts, then plant outdoors.

Harvest from early summer.

Garlic is well worth growing, as you can plant a clove from an existing bulb and you are away. Probably the most useful flavouring vegetable you can grow other than onions and herbs.

EAT

Cook by frying, caramelising, barbecuing on a skewer, or deep fry rings in batter. Cut onion into wedges and roast it or bake one for 20-30 minutes until tender. Onions are great to stuff with a vegan sausage filling.

Pissaladiere is a French onion tart with a base a bit like a pizza.

Ingredients
200g flour
2 tsp yeast
1 tbsp oil
Topping:
I tbsp oil
Ikg onions
Tin of tomatoes
Garlic cloves crushed
Handful of olives
Herbs such as thyme

Method
Mix flour, salt and yeast in a bowl and add water and oil to make into a dough. Roll it out and press it into an oiled baking tin. Fry the onions and add the tomatoes, garlic and herbs and simmer for 45 minutes. Then spread the mix on the dough, decorate with olives and bake for 30 minutes at 220C/Gas mark 7.

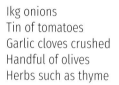

PAK CHOI/BOX CHOI/CHINESE CABBAGE

Winter hardy and great nutritionally.

· Folates	66 µg	16%
· Pyridoxine	0.194 mg	15%
· Riboflavin	0.070 mg	5%
· Vitamin A	4468 IU	149%
· Vitamin C	45 mg	75%
· Vitamin K	45.5 µg	38%
· Sodium	65 mg	4%
· Potassium	252 mg	5%
· Calcium	105 mg	10.5%
· Iron	0.80 mg	10%
· Magnesium	19 mg	5%
· Manganese	0.159 mg	7%
· Phosphorus	37 mg	5%

GROW

Sow outdoors May-August and water well. Watch out for bolting (running to seed).

(M4rtine Pixabay)

EAT

Eat as baby leaf or in salads and stir fries as mature leaves, or as miso pak choi tofu soup. Place miso paste in a large pan and cover with 800ml boiling water. Mix and simmer. Add chilli, ginger, tofu and mushrooms to the pan and simmer for about five minutes until the mushrooms have softened. Stir in noodles, pak choi and spring onions and simmer for two minutes. Heat a frying pan and dry-fry sesame seeds for 3-4 mins until golden to use as a garnish.

PARSNIP

A fantastic root vegetable to grow. Easier than carrots and with more flavour than potatoes, distinguishing the roast parsnip from the roast spud during Sunday dinner is always a challenge.

NUTRITION

· Carbohydrates	17.99 g	14%
· Dietary Fibre	4.9 g	13%
· Folates	67 µg	17%
· Pantothenic acid	0.600 mg	12%
· Vitamin C	17 mg	29%
· Vitamin K	22.5 µg	19%
· Potassium	375 mg	8%
· Copper	0.120 mg	13%
· Iron	0.59 mg	7.5%
· Magnesium	29 mg	7%
· Manganese	0.560 mg	24%
· Phosphorus	71 mg	10%
· Zinc	0.59 mg	5%

GROW

Sow outdoors February-May in prepared seed bed, thinly. Cover with 1.5cm of soil. Thin so 20cm apart and harvest in winter.

EAT

Cook by roasting or use as a cake ingredient. If you add 500g of grated parsnips to a cake it adds flavour and sweetness, as well as moisture and fragrance, in the same way as you could add carrot, beetroot or courgette to a classic cake mix.

Ingredients
175g sultanas
150g self-raising flour
150g white flour
175g sugar
200ml oil
Spices
Icing
150g icing sugar
200g vegan margarine
Vanilla essence

Method
Pre-heat the oven to 190C/gas mark 5.
Stir the dry ingredients together then mix in the oil and 200ml water and put into a greased tin. Bake for 45 minutes then turn down the oven 30C/ to gas mark 3 and cook for a further 30 minutes. Leave to cool.
Mix the icing ingredients and spread on the cooled cake.

Caption for this saying what it is.
(Alexas-fotos Pixabay)

PEA

Freezing and canning have made this vegetable lose its unique fresh appeal for many people. However, mushy peas (best bought tinned or from the chip shop) cannot be surpassed (although pease pudding is truly a dish for discerning palates).

NUTRITION

· Carbohydrates	14.45 g	11%
· Protein	5.42 g	10%
· Dietary Fibre	5.1 g	13%
· Folates	65 µg	16%
· Niacin	2.090 mg	13%
· Pyridoxine	0.169 mg	13%
· Riboflavin	0.132 mg	10%
· Thiamin	0.266 mg	22%
· Vitamin A	765 IU	25.5%
· Vitamin C	40 mg	67%
· Vitamin K	24.8 µg	21%
· Copper	0.176 mg	20%
· Iron	1.47 mg	18%
· Magnesium	33 mg	8%
· Manganese	0.410 mg	18%
· Zinc	1.24 mg	11%

GROW

Peas don't mind cooler weather. Sow seed direct in a place where you can provide support of twiggy sticks or wire netting for pea tendrils to climb up. Net to protect seed from birds. Mulch and water. Don't feed peas with nitrogen rich fertilisers as this can cause lots of leafy growth instead of producing pea pods.

EAT

Eat fresh and raw, boiled, or as a puree.

To make a pea puree, cook peas in a pan of boiling water for 2 to 3 minutes or until tender. Drain. Brown onion and garlic and combine with the peas and oil or vegan cream. Process until smooth and season.

PEPPER

(Sweet/Bell/Capsicum/Chilli)

Another tough one to grow without heated indoor space. Riper greens and reds have more vitamin C than yellows. Try chilli peppers grown for flavour and not just heat.

NUTRITION

· Dietary Fibre	2.1 g	5.5%
· Folates	46 µg	12%
· Niacin	0.979 mg	6%
· Pyridoxine	0.291 mg	22%
· Riboflavin	0.085 mg	6.5%
· Vitamin A	3131 IU	101%
· Vitamin C	127.7 mg	213%
· Vitamin E	1.58 mg	11%
· Iron	0.43 mg	5%
· Manganese	0.112 mg	5%

GROW

Buy young ready-grown plants in the spring, but don't place them outside until June as they are frost tender. Seeds need to be sown in late-February or early March at 20°C. Ideally grow them in a greenhouse. You may need a propagator to get seeds to germinate. Plant young plants in the ground under glass by mid-May. Or you can keep them in pots and place them outside in early June. You can use grow bags too. Feed with fertiliser. Remember a 15-10-5 fertiliser contains 15% nitrogen, 10% phosphorus, and 5% potassium. Higher phosphate and potassium number will encourage more fruit production. A lower nitrogen number will help the plant grow, without doing it at the expense of producing fruit.

The related chilli peppers are also

· Potassium	425 mg	9%
· Iron	0.81 mg	10%
· Magnesium	23 mg	6%
· Manganese	0.141mg	6%
· Phosphorus	57 mg	8%

GROW

Buy seed potatoes and allow to 'chit' or grow shoots. Plant 12cm deep and 30cm apart in spring for 'earlies'. When leaves reach 20cm, 'earth up' soil around them to protect from frost and light, which makes potatoes green and poisonous. Wait for flowers, then harvest earlies in June, with later plantings in succession after that.

well worth growing as they add so much flavour to food and take up little space. Sow the small fiery capsicum variety indoors 0.5cm deep thinly in compost in temperatures of 15-20 degrees C. Keep moist. Seedlings appear after 7-21 days. Transplant to individual pots when large enough to handle to grow on. You can then plant outside in larger pots. Choose varieties for flavour, not just heat. Chillies contain a chemical called capsaicin that stimulates the nerve endings in the mucous membranes, making them taste hot, measured on the Scoville scale.

EAT

Roast sliced bell peppers in oil. Eat raw in salad. Stuff with cooked rice, vegan cheese, onions, and herbs. To make chilli oil, hang up chilli peppers to dry. Heat oil and add broken up dried peppers. For a cold infusion, add broken up chilli peppers to cold oil and leave to steep.

POTATO

The easiest vegetable to grow. Lost favour because of pasta and rice, but don't ignore the most versatile, and surprisingly nutritious, spud. Potatoes contain all nine amino acids. I love growing potatoes. You just stick them in the ground under the soil (or in a soil-filled bucket or bag) and wait.

NUTRITION

· Energy	77 Kcal	4%
· Carbohydrates	17.49 g	13%
· Protein	2.05 g	4%
· Dietary Fibre	2.1 g	5%
· Niacin	1.061 mg	6%
· Pantothenic acid	0.279 mg	6%
· Pyridoxine	0.298 mg	23%
· Thiamin	0.081 mg	7%
· Vitamin C	19.7 mg	33%

Mash, chips, wedges, baked, fried, sautéed, roast, dauphinoise, Jerseys in salads. Potato shortbread is surprisingly good.

Ingredients
75g margarine
50g sugar
100g mashed potato
100g flour
pinch salt

Method
Mix the ingredients together thoroughly, roll and bake for 10 minutes at 180C/Gas mark 4.

PUMPKIN

We used to cut holes in turnips for Halloween. Now the US pumpkin is ubiquitous worldwide on 31 October and beyond, and that's no bad thing. The pumpkin is versatile, fun to grow and its seeds are nutritious too. Don't waste the flesh for the sake of being the most ghoulish gourd.

NUTRITION

· Carbohydrates	6.50 g	5%
· Pantothenic acid	0.298 mg	6%
· Pyridoxine	0.061 mg	5%
· Riboflavin	0.110 mg	8.5%
· Vitamin A	7384 IU	246%
· Vitamin C	9.0 mg	15%
· Vitamin E	1.06 mg	7%
· Potassium	340 mg	7%
· Copper	0.127 mg	14%
· Iron	0.80 mg	10%
· Phosphorus	44mg	5%

Pumpkin seeds are high in calories; about 559 calories per 100g. Also, they are packed with fibre, vitamins, minerals, protein (30g/100g or 54% RDA) and numerous health promoting antioxidants. The seeds are an excellent source of amino acid tryptophan and glutamate. Tryptophan is converted into serotonin and niacin. Serotonin is a beneficial neurochemical, while tryptophan is the precursor of B-complex vitamin, niacin (60 mg of tryptophan = 1 mg).

Pumpkin seeds are a very good source of antioxidant vitamin-E; contain about 35.10 mg of tocopherol-gamma per 100 g (about 237% of RDA). Furthermore, its seeds contain good amounts of essential minerals like copper, manganese,

potassium, calcium, iron, magnesium, zinc, and selenium. The seeds are best from mature pumpkins which are good roasted.

GROW

Grow pumpkins from seed indoors from April, or outdoors from late May after the last frost in the spot where they are to grow. They like sun and fertile soil. Place straw under them as they swell to stop any chance of rotting. Underplanting works well beneath pumpkins.

EAT

Roast or use in cakes.
To make pumpkin hummus, whizz roast pumpkin with garlic, olive oil, lemon juice, tahini paste and chickpeas.

(Jai79 Pixabay)

QUINOA

Growable and astonishing good for you, quinoa is another real superfood that was not available until recent years. Quinoa is grain-like but related to the spinach, chard and beet family. Quinoa is able to survive high altitudes, thin and cold air, hot sun, salty or sandy soil, little rainfall, and sub-freezing temperatures, so they don't need much water and fit into a low-irrigation xeriscaping scheme.

NUTRITION

· Energy	368 Kcal	18.5%
· Carbohydrates	64.16 g	49%
· Protein	14.12 g	35%
· Total Fat	6.07 g	20%

· Dietary Fibre	7 g	18.5%
· Folates (B9)	184 µg	46%
· Niacin (B3)	1.520 mg	9.5%
· Riboflavin (B2)	0.318 mg	24%
· Thiamin (B1)	0.360 mg	30%
· Vitamin E	2.44 mg	17%
· Potassium	563 mg	12%
· Copper	0.590 mg	65.5%
· Iron	4.57 mg	57%
· Magnesium	197 mg	42%
· Manganese	2.003 mg	87%
· Phosphorus	457 mg	65%
· Selenium	8.5 µg	15%
· Zinc	3.10 mg	28%

GROW

Start seeds in small pots and then plant them outside in late May spaced 60cm apart. By August, stake them because they will reach up to 2m tall. Harvest in September when the first grains fall.

(Einladung-Zum-Essen Pixabay)

EAT

Processing is the hard bit. Rub the seed heads over a soil sieve to get the grains out. Place the grains in a fine-meshed strainer and run cold water over the quinoa while rubbing the seeds together in your hands to remove the bitter taste.

Cook like rice to go with curries, stews and tagines.

RADISH

Radish is a neat little crop for growing in small spaces. Kids can grow it and there are plenty of varieties to try, including mooli, daikon and watermelon radishes.

NUTRITION

· Folates	25 μg	6%
· Pyridoxine	0.071 mg	5.5%
· Vitamin C	14.8 mg	25%
· Vitamin E	0 mg	9%
· Potassium	233 mg	5%
· Copper	0.050 mg	5%

GROW

Sow seed like any salad where they are to crop, indoor or out. They grow quickly. Harvest before they get woody.

EAT

Radish are peppery and crisp. Add to salads.

RASPBERRIES

My favourite berry to grow. They do well all year and the sweet flavour is amazing for something that is good for you, often even champagne-like.

NUTRITION

· Carbohydrates	11.94 g	9%
· Dietary Fibre	6.5 g	16%
· Folates	21 μg	5%
· Vitamin C	26.2 mg	47%
· Vitamin E	1.42 mg	9%
· Vitamin K	7.8 μg	6.5%
· Copper	90 μg	10%
· Iron	0.69 mg	8.5%
· Magnesium	22 mg	5.5%
· Manganese	0.670 mg	29%

GROW

Raspberries and other cane fruits such as blackberries and hybrids like tayberries and loganberries. Buy canes and plant them. Ideally support them on posts and wires and cover to protect from birds.

EAT

Jam if they squash. Juice if they are even squashier. Eat fresh if they are intact by the time you get them home.

NUTRITION

· Dietary Fibre	2.2 g	6%
· Folates	194 µg	48.5%
· Pyridoxine	0.195 mg	15%
· Riboflavin	0.189 mg	14.5%
· Thiamin	0.078 mg	6.5%
· Vitamin A	9377 IU	312%
· Vitamin C	28.1 mg	47%
· Vitamin E	2.03 mg	13.5%
· Vitamin K	482.9 µg	402%
· Sodium	79 mg	5%
· Potassium	558 mg	12%
· Calcium	99 mg	10%
· Copper	0.130 mg	14%
· Iron	2.71 mg	34%

RHUBARB

Unjustly maligned as an old-fashioned boring British pudding crop, rhubarb is in fact a vegetable that is very tough and will come back year after year with little nurturing and will give you fresh stems that have a fizzy flavour and nutritional kick to rival the raspberry.

NUTRITION

· Dietary Fibre	1.8 g	5%
· Vitamin C	8 mg	13%
· Vitamin K	29.3 µg	24%
· Potassium	288 mg	6%
· Calcium	86 mg	8.5%
· Manganese	0.196 mg	8.5%

GROW

Buy a 'crown' (root) and plant in a sunny place with fertile soil in late autumn, or plant pot-grown rhubarb anytime. Harvest in the second year and don't harvest after mid-summer as stems get woody and the plant needs foliage to build up food reserves for next year.

EAT

Flavours that pair well with rhubarb are vanilla, ginger, orange and star anise.

Rhubarb is usually roasted or stewed with sugar, agave syrup or soft sweet fruits and cooked rhubarb is often combined with (vegan) cream in a panna cotta or trifle. Put under a crumble topping or alongside a posset, or make a sorbet. Puree this fruit and add a little sugar, and that's your sorbet base. Simmer equal parts sugar and water until the sugar is dissolved and let it cool. Then freeze.

SPINACH

Always portrayed as the healthiest vegetable, spinach has fallen behind new dark green superfoods such as kale in recent years. But this is a great crop to grow and is incredibly healthy.

Magnesium	79 mg	20%
Manganese	0.897 mg	39%
Zinc	0.53 mg	5%

GROW

Get the soil right and you should have no problems with spinach. As with many other crops, the soil needs to be well manured and fertilised – which the veganic system will guarantee.

Sow seed outdoors 2.5cm deep and with rows 30cm apart in spring for baby leaf or leave to grow into mature plants if you thin out. You can grow spinach in containers. Sow seeds of summer cultivars every few weeks from February (under fleece or cloches), or outdoors from mid-March to the end of May. You can also sow winter varieties under cover of a cloche, fleece or straw.

EAT

Boil or sauté as quickly as possible so as not to lose nutrients.

SPROUTING SEEDS

Go beyond mustard and cress by resurrecting this indoor staple.

GROW

Mustard and cress were often the first plants we grew on windowsills as children, in yoghurt pots or on damp tissue paper.

Continue that tradition by sprouting seeds or beans, such as any legumes. These include alfalfa, radish, green lentils, broccoli, chickpeas and fenugreek on window ledges (or anywhere at room temperatures - they even sprout in the dark).

Soak the seeds or beans for a day, then rinse and drain them once a day. They soon sprout in a day or two.

Mung beans and lentils are the easiest to sprout.

The sprouts need air so place in a container such as a plastic pot with a cloth or paper towel secured over it with a rubber band. Or use a jam jar with small holes in the lid.

Soak some seeds in the jar for 12 hours so they swell. Rinse and drain through the cloth/lid. Repeat every 12 hours until the sprouts are ready, which takes 2-4 days.

You can also buy mini-greenhouse germinators.

EAT

Cook in stir fries or use small quantities raw.

lamifranquoi

Nonnatthapat

STRAWBERRIES

One of the most sought-after fruits, yet one of the easiest to grow. Strawberries always make people smile.

NUTRITION

- Carbohydrates   7.7 g   6%
- Dietary Fibre   2.0 g   5%
- Folates   24 µg   6%
- Vitamin C   58.8 mg   98%
- Iron   0.41 mg   5%
- Manganese   0.386 mg   17%

GROW

Plant root-like 'runners' in late spring or early autumn, or finished plants in autumn somewhere sunny, with shelter and fertile, well-drained soil, containers, or grow-bags.

EAT

Don't cook unless you have to make jam from squashed strawberries. Don't add sugar either if you want to taste the full flavour.

SUNFLOWER SEEDS

Sunflowers are the most spectacular flowers to grow. Plant one for each family member and see which grows tallest. My record is a relatively modest 4.5m. The sweet and nutty seeds are the wonderful payback at the end of the season for the feeding and staking that sunflowers need to thrive. The seeds are full of essential fatty acids, vitamins and minerals. Birds love them too.

NUTRITION

- Energy   584 Kcal   29%
- Carbohydrates   20 g   15%
- Protein   20.78 g   37%
- Total Fat   51.46 g   172%
- Dietary Fibre   8.6 g   23%
- Folates   227 µg   57%
- Niacin   8.335 mg   52%

· Iron	5.25 mg	63%
· Magnesium	325 mg	81%
· Manganese	1.950 mg	85%
· Phosphorus	660 mg	94%
· Selenium	53 µg	96%
· Zinc	5.00 mg	45%

GROW

You need a sunny, sheltered spot. Plant 45cm apart in 3cm deep holes. Fertilise, water, stake and mulch. Or start off indoors and transplant outside.

EAT

Eat sunflower seeds whole, raw or cooked. You can either boil them for an hour in water or roast them. To roast, cover seeds in a bowl with water and allow to soak overnight. Add salt to taste. Drain, then spread them flat, with no overlaps, on a baking sheet on a tray and oven bake for 40 minutes. Add to the top of bread, loaves and cakes, or sprinkle into salads or over breakfast cereals.

· Pantothenic acid	1.130 mg	22%
· Pyridoxine	1.345 mg	103%
· Riboflavin	0.355 mg	27%
· Thiamin	1.480 mg	123%
· Vitamin E	35.17 mg	234%
· Potassium	645 mg	14%
· Calcium	78 mg	8%
· Copper	1.800 mg	200%

SWEDE/TURNIP

Yet another hideously neglected vegetable that is simple to grow and has plenty of vitamin C and minerals. Radish-sized baby turnips are sweet and peppery and are not grown or eaten enough except in fancy restaurants.

NUTRITION

·Carbohydrates	6.43 g	5%
· Dietary Fibre	1.8 g	5%
· Pyridoxine	0.090 mg	7%
· Vitamin C	21 mg	35%
· Potassium	233 mg	5%
· Copper	0.085 mg	9%
· Iron	0.30 mg	4%
· Manganese	0.134 mg	6%

GROW

Sow outside directly where they are to grow because they do not transplant well. Sow from late winter to early

summer. Cover with fleece to keep off flea beetles. Pull them when they are golf ball to orange-sized. If bigger, they get woody. Lift turnips before winter.

EAT

Eat turnip leaves or make into alternative Halloween lanterns. Roast like pumpkin or other root veg or mash with potatoes and black pepper. Turnips are more peppery than swedes. Baby turnips just need washing and lightly boiling while mature turnips are usually peeled before cooking, for up to 50 minutes. They can also be stuffed. Swedes are more delicate than turnips and should be diced then boiled or steamed for 10-15 minutes only, or roasted for 40 minutes.

SWEETCORN

Difficult to grow well. Corn on the cob, frozen and tinned sweetcorn means home grown can look like a poor substitute. Nice to have success with though.

NUTRITION

· Energy	86Kcal	4%
· Carbohydrates	18.70 g	14%
· Folates	42 µg	10.5%
· Niacin	1.770 mg	11%
· Pantothenic acid	0.717 mg	14%
· Pyridoxine	0.093 mg	7%
· Thiamin	0.155 mg	13%
· Vitamin A	187 IU	6%
· Vitamin C	6.8 mg	11%
· Potassium	270 mg	6%
· Copper	0.054 mg	6%
· Iron	0.52 mg	6.5%

· Magnesium	37 mg	9%
· Manganese	0.163 mg	7%
· Zinc	0.46 mg	4%

GROW

Sow indoors in pots and plant out after the last frosts. You can plant direct in warm areas. Grow in blocks of 4x4 to ensure good pollination, 40cm apart. When the tassels turn brown, peel back the husk to check the corn and if it is going yellow, it's ready.

EAT

On the cob, barbecued, as a side, sweetcorn is a versatile vegetable. Put a cob under the grill coated in a little oil or use raw in salads. Boil or steam, or sautee. Deep fry fritters in a vegan batter mix or add to soup. Vegan batter is simply a mix of flour and salt with water stirred in and 1tsp of baking powder or soda added for body.

SWEET POTATO

The orange and purple colours of sweet potatoes signify beat-carotene – and vast amounts of vitamin A for the immune system, skin and eyes. Little-grown until recent years, this root vegetable is now much admired for its nutritional value, though it can be tough to grow.

NUTRITION

· Energy	86 Kcal	4%
· Carbohydrates	20.12 g	15.5%
· Dietary Fibre	3 g	8%
· Pantothenic acid	0.80 mg	16%
· Pyridoxine	0.209 mg	15%
· Riboflavin	0.061 mg	5.5%
· Thiamin	0.078 mg	6.5%
· Vitamin A	14187 IU	473%
· Potassium	337 mg	7%
· Iron	0.61 mg	7.5%
· Magnesium	25 mg	6%
· Manganese	0.258 mg	11%
· Phosphorus	47 mg	7%

GROW

Sweet potatoes are grown from 'slips' - long shoots that have been removed from 'chitted' sweet potato tubers. The reason they have been little grown is because sweet potatoes need high temperatures of 21-26°C. So plant in greenhouse borders, polytunnels or under cloches or through a sheet of black polythene to warm the soil. Thy need deep soil and plenty of space to spread above ground. After 12-16 weeks, when foliage is dying back, you can harvest the tubers.

EAT

Roast, mash, stuff, roast, wedges – all the things you would do with a potato.

TOMATOES

The most popular crop for the home gardener to grow because home grown taste better; are satisfying to grow and good value.

NUTRITION

· Pyridoxine	0.080 mg	6%
· Vitamin A	833 IU	28%
· Vitamin C	13 mg	21.5%
· Vitamin K	7.9 µg	6.5%
· Potassium	237 mg	5%
· Manganese	0.15 mg	6.5%

GROW

Sow indoors January-April and plant out April-June. Sow 0.5cm deep thinly in a pot of compost. Keep at 15-20°C. Transplant to individual pots when 10-15cm tall. Grow on in cooler conditions, then plant out. Support by tying to canes and pinch it side shoots and then growing tip after 5-6 trusses of tomatoes have set. Blight is an issue in cold and wet seasons. Avoid by growing under glass/indoors.

EAT

It's something of a waste to cook home grown tomatoes so use in salads with dressings. Or if they are green and won't ripen by the end of summer, make chutney:

Ingredients
600g of green tomatoes
175g sugar
150ml white wine vinegar
Bunch of shallots
Handful of sultanas
Ginger, chilli to taste

Method
Heat the sugar in a frying pan until the sugar melts and caramelises. Add the white wine vinegar, shallots, garlic, ginger, chilli, sultanas and green tomatoes and bring to the boil. Simmer for one hour until the chutney has thickened then pour into sterilised jars.
Or blend to use as a pizza topping.

Ingredients

300g plain flour
I tsp yeast
1 tsp sugar
I tsp olive oil
100g tomato sauce
Handful of any chopped veg

Method

Knead the plain flour, 250ml water, fast action dried yeast, sugar, ½ tsp salt and 1 tbsp olive oil for the base dough. Leave for 30 minutes to prove under cling film. Pat into rounds and place on greased baking sheets. Spread tomato sauce and add chopped veg. Bake for 15-20 minutes.

VINES

(Grapes)

Grapes and wine – both symbols of the good life. Everyone has happy memories of vineyards visited on holiday. Vague memories, but happy ones. Growing grapes can add interest to your plot. And you can expect to produce table grapes (if grown in a greenhouse because they need more warmth to get sweet enough to eat raw) and even, perhaps, plonk.

NUTRITION

- Carbohydrates — 18 g — 14%
- Pyridoxine — 0.086 mg — 7.5%
- Riboflavin — 0.070 mg — 5%
- Thiamin — 0.069 mg — 6%
- Vitamin C — 10.8 mg — 18%
- Vitamin K — 14.6 μg — 12%
- Copper — 0.127 mg — 14%

GROW

Growing decent grapes is difficult and takes horticultural skill. You will need a south-facing fence. Plant autumn or spring.

You need to support the vines with wires. Stretch horizontal galvanised wires 30cm apart and attached to vine eye - long, metal supports bent at one end to form a hole to run the wire through and are fixed to the wall using a drill. If you aren't growing next to a fence or wall, attach your wires to posts.

Dig a hole in sandy or stony soil, bigger than the root ball of the vine, 15cm away from your fence or wall. Add manure and grit into the hole. Space plants 1.5m apart.

Pruning is the hardest and most complicated part. There is no no-nonsense method.

In winter of year one, prune the new vine to within two buds of the bottom. When buds come out in spring, remove the top bud leaving the remaining one to grow, tied to the wires vertically. Chop side shoots.

In spring of year two let three side shoots grow, then in autumn chop the top stem to three buds and train the other two shoots to either side and tie to a horizontal wire.

In year three train the side shoots vertically to the wires and hope they bear fruit. Feed with potash to help. After harvest, cut the two branches back to the main stem. Then cut the new centre shoot back to three buds and the two side shoots tied in to replace the branches that fruited.

If the crop fails, at least you get nice leaf colour in the autumn.

EAT

Raw or make your own wine or sell your grapes to a communal press and contribute to your community wine vintage or set up your own communal press if there isn't one locally.

(Couleur Pixabay)

OTHER CROPS/
MUSHROOMS

Mushrooms are useful mineral sources and are a good substitute for meat in many dishes. They are also growable at home with a bit of effort.

NUTRITION

- Copper 0.3g 15% RDA
- Selenium 9mcg 14%
- Phosphorus 90mcg 9%
- Potassium 330mcg 9%

GROW

Spawn and a moist, humid atmosphere are the key ingredients to mushroom growing.

Sow outside from spring to August on lawns. Lift turf and spread spores. Replace turf. Water. Spread spores on your compost heap in summer. Harvest in 10-12 weeks.

Inside, grow year-round, in any dark place such as a cellar, shed, cupboard or garage, or in a greenhouse in the spring or autumn. Ideal temperature is 16°C. Use 50g of spores to spawn 0.25m2. Yields are best if you use mushroom compost made from straw, rich compost and lime. But old rotting straw, plain straw and rich manure all work. Hope for three or more crops. Cover in damp newspaper. After 14-21 days, when white mycelium threads appear, remove the paper and 'case' in 3cm of half soil/half compost with a couple of handfuls of lime for alkalinity. Or you could also use half compost and half chalk or lime... Keep moist and wait a month for mushrooms to grow.

Growing mushrooms on logs involves using dowels which are impregnated with mushroom mycelium (mushroom spawn). Hammer up to 15 dowels flush into drilled holes in a 10-15cm diameter, 50cm long hardwood log. Use oak, beech, birch, hazel, willow. Keep the logs shaded from direct sunlight and strong winds to prevent them drying out before use. Drill holes 15cm apart down the length of the log and 7cm apart around the diameter of the log. Seal the inoculation holes with wax. Put the logs underground, in a shady place or wrap in a bin bag. Wait 6-18 months. When the mushrooms appear, move to a warm, sheltered, moist area in dappled shade such as woodland to fruit. Logs will be productive for four to six years.

Indoors, grow oyster mushrooms in straw in six weeks, all year round. Pour boiling water on bagged straw, leave to cool, drain, sprinkle spawn on the straw and shake. Seal the bag and put in a warm 18-25°C environment such as a cistern cupboard for a month. Then move to a 10-15°C environment for three to five days.

Remove the straw from the growing bag, place it in the fruiting tray and cover the straw with the perforated fruiting bag to encourage mushrooms to develop. Place the straw in a lit area but shaded from direct sun, at a temperature of 10-21°C. Spray the straw with water twice a day as the mushrooms begin to develop. Mushrooms should be harvested within 10 days, before the caps unfurl and release their spores. After harvesting the crop, the straw can be soaked in cold water for two hours before returning it to the fruiting tray and repositioning the fruiting bag. Again, place the straw in a lit area at a temperature of 10-21°C. Repeat this process until the straw is exhausted.

EAT

Avoid soaking as they absorb water and will not brown when cooking. Brush mushrooms instead to clean them then coat them in oil and roast, coat in batter and breadcrumbs and fry in hot oil, stir fry with soy sauce and oil, grill until brown with optional marinades, or sauté in oil until brown.

(Aitoff Pix)

SEAWEED

Seaweed is a magic ingredient in cooking and gardening, giving large amounts of nutrition with a small dose. Adding seaweed fertiliser products to your plants may be simpler than harvesting or growing your own.

NUTRITION

- Vitamin K 66mcg 82%
- Folate 180mcg 45%
- Magnesium 120mcg 30%
- Calcium 170mcg 17%
- Iron 3mcg 16%

GROW

You can't grow seaweed without an extensive aquaponics system, but it is possible to grow your own seaweed at home in a large aquarium in a sunny place filled with salt water boiled up, one teaspoon of salt per gallon of water heated to 27C. Provide an anchor for the seaweed with a large rock on the bottom of the aquarium, which should have water at about 22°F. Attach to the rock by the 'roots' (base). Add 50ml liquid fertiliser into the aquarium to provide nutrients for the seaweed. Spirulina is a similar source of protein. I'd suggest simply harvesting seaweed from the beach, cutting 15cm from where it attaches. This makes for a sustainable crop.

EAT

Nori seaweed is good to wrap sushi. Kombu (a kelp) or wakame is good in miso soup. Chinese restaurants call deep fried spring cabbage crispy seaweed, but you can use real, fresh or dried and rehydrated seaweed to deep fry. Dried dulse is good in curries, soup, bread, salad or as a snack.

TRUFFLES

Foodies love these intensely-flavoured delicacies, and they cost loads. They are growable, with time, space and effort.

· Potassium	754mg	21%
· Protein	9g	18%
· Iron	7mcg	32%
· Calcium	150mg	15%
· Magnesium	80mg	20%

GROW

For truffles, plant truffle trees, which are hazelnut trees that have been inoculated with the truffle fungus. Truffles (not the chocolate type) are a type of mushroom that grow on the roots of hazel and oak throughout Europe. When people in the UK used to talk about truffles, they almost always meant chocolate. Nowadays, awareness of these fascinating native fungi is growing quickly and so is the interest in the truffle trees. Home growers range from people who have a couple of trees in a back garden to those who have filled whole allotments.

Fresh truffles are harvested from July to November and are valued for their distinctive flavour. Truffles are used to flavour many dishes and to make oils.

Buy young hazel trees impregnated with the truffle fungus. Good trees won't suffer from contamination to ensure success in a shorter time, with higher yield and reliability. Truffles should be produced three-four years after planting. Late winter or early spring is a good time to plant trees. Most of England has

a suitable climate and the soil should ideally have a pH of around 7.3-7.9. A typical plant should produce about 1kg of truffles per year on average after four-six years. They can live for 50 years. Hazelnut trees are hardy, native plants, suitable for any garden size as they can be pruned. They like lime. The hazel tree is also a great wildlife tree. Buy 30cm trees. Plant densely or your truffles may suffer from under-colonisation. The hazelnut trees used to cultivate truffles will produce nuts. See www.plantationsystems.com to source suitable trees. You can use oaks too. The hazel trees can be pruned to keep them quite small where as if the oaks grow too big for most plots.

Truffles don't expect too much water or fertiliser. Grow lavender among the trees. Finding them is half the fun. Traditionally pigs or dogs dug them up. They grow just under the soil's surface. Coppice the trees – regular cutting leads to better growth.

EAT

Cook truffle risotto. If you've never tried truffle then a good introduction is to try some of the truffle-infused olive-oil and drizzle it on mashed potato.

FORAGING

Foraging is trendy, but finding food in wild places has been mankind's staple since time began. The easiest foraging of all is blackberry picking.

GROW

Brambles flourish, like seagulls, nettles and grey squirrels, when other, less cherished living things struggle. They are tolerant of most soil types and are a pesky weed on public ground and in private gardens. You can also grow your own blackberries if you haven't been scared off by wild blackberries' scary invasiveness. But why bother when brambles are so widespread?

Though they are a weed in the garden, or allotment, brambles are simple to remove. Cut back using secateurs (wear tough gloves). Lift the root ball with a fork. It comes out satisfyingly cleanly. Leave plant and roots to dry, then burn or compost.

Folklore says blackberries should not be picked after Old Michelmas

BLACKBERRY JUICE.
Method
Crush through a sieve with the back of a spoon into a wide container. Chuck the leftover seeds. The juice can be a bit tart. Or add a bit of sugar. You only need 10ml or so to satisfy them. Full of vitamin C.

Blackberry crunch: Add a sprinkle of granola into a portion of juice. Add vegan crème fraiche and stir.

Blackberry and apple pie. The classic dish.

Ingredients
175g plain flour
100g vegan butter
25g caster sugar
300g cooking apples
225g blackberries
100g sugar to make the fruit filling sweet. Extras for the pastry are one tsp grated lemon zest, vegan egg and soya milk, to moisten and glaze.

Method
Heat oven to 180C or Gas mark 4. Sift flour and salt into a bowl. Cut butter into small pieces and rub in until mixture resembles breadcrumbs. Mix in the sugar, lemon, vegan egg and soya milk to form dough. Knead.

Put apples and blackberries into a one litre pie dish, and then sprinkle sugar over. Roll out the pastry on a floured surface then cover the pie dish with it and seal the edges. Bake for 40 minutes until golden. Serve with vegan ice cream.

Blackberry Smoothie
A great way to introduce more protein into a vegan diet. Blitz 12-15 blackberries with 150g silken tofu and 100g soya milk. Sweeten to taste with your preferred sweetener.

Foraging may not seem the normal thing to do on a cultivated area such as a plot but there is plenty of wild food growing on the fringes, if you look. Not only that, but on the way to and from the plot there will be wild food to forage. Autumn is the traditional time for harvest, when the results of hard graft on the allotment and in the fields are reaped. Mixing foraged with home-grown food has become the most low-carbon and sustainable 'lifestyle' choice. But could it be that the hedgerows near you have been stripped by people taking up the nature's bounty trend in the recession? The reason why gardeners don't grow dandelions or fat hen is because they are weeds that spread out of control too easily. So make controlled 'cultivations' of wild food such as nettles, brambles and various weeds to harvest from your plot.

Here's a foraged food top ten from plants that should be plentiful in autumn:
- elder (cordial, cakes, fritters)
- fat hen (spinach-like weed)
- nettle (soup), dog rose (jam/tea)
- dandelion (salad leaves/boiled roots)
- blackberry (and apple pie)
- cherry (jam/raw)
- beech nuts
- sweet chestnuts (oil/raw)
- apples (obvious)

For elderflower cordial, mix 1kg sugar, one litre boiling water, 20 flowerheads, a lemon, 25g citric acid.

Rosehips (syrup), sloes (gin), walnuts and hazelnuts are also useful; all wild foods that might be growing near your plot.

Day (11 October) because the devil has claimed them. He often has, in the form of botrytis mould on ageing fruits subjected to colder weather.

So get in early, late in the UK summer.

Don't pick low down – there's a dog wee risk.

Only go for the blackest, ripest jewels. Anything lighter purple, orangey or green will be sour. Over-ripe is fine but will squash. The mess of blackberries is hard to handle.

EAT

When you get them home, take the bowls straight to the sink and rinse. Pick out the best ones for eating as single fruits. They cost the same as raspberries and strawberries in supermarkets. Pick out the stalks and green ones. Mushier fruits can be mashed through a sieve to make juice. Use the back of a spoon. Foraged bilberries work equally well.

GLUTS

To avoid a glut, only plant a little of everything. Plant half a metre of lettuce and not a full packet. Plant early, mid and late season potatoes to spread out your harvests. But if the weather is right, you will have too much of something every year to eat before it goes off. So the crop

Add sugar to fruit.

needs preserving. The rest of the glut gets frozen in a chest freezer in the garage. Back in the 1970s *Good Life* era there were loads of books on 'deep freezing' (like there were on using microwaves a decade later). There were also plenty of books on 'preserves and condiments'. A generation later, the advice on making jam and chutney is back, this time via TV and on the internet.

Making jam is the best way to deal with a glut of fruit. Crab apples, blackcurrants, gooseberries, plums, redcurrants, cooking apples, cranberries, damsons, quince, oranges, lemons, plums, raspberries, loganberries, boysenberries, tayberries and apricots, blackberries, blueberries, strawberries, rhubarb, elderberries, peaches, sweet cherries, apples, pears, figs and marrow are all possibilities. Use a big stainless-steel pan.

Every fruit needs slightly different treatment. For blackcurrants, gently heat the fruit (frozen is fine) for about an hour in water. Add the same amount of sugar and stir until it dissolves. Boil rapidly for 10

Stir over a low heat.

minutes for a couple of jars-worth or longer if you have more. Skim scum at the end. When the jam reaches 105°C (220°F), it is set. Test by putting a teaspoonful onto a cold plate. Push the outer edge of the jam puddle into the centre with your index finger. If the jam wrinkles it will set. Or just hold the plate upside down and hope the jam doesn't fall to the floor. If the jam is over boiled the mixture will be too sticky. Under done is worse as it is just fruity, sugary water. When the jam has reached the proper setting point, jug it out, pour it into sterilised (cleaned in boiling water and thoroughly dried or 'cooked' in the oven for 10 minutes) jars and cover with a lid immediately.

ALTERNATIVE IDEAS

• **Pickle**. Choose crunchy and raw veg such as onions, cauliflower or beetroot. Quickly boil (one minute). Use white wine vinegar and pure pickling salt. Put in a jar, seal. Refrigerate. Sauerkraut is an option

Decant into sterilised jars.

too. Salt cabbage and the released brine ferments over a week pickling the veg when left in an airtight jar. Also try piccalilli.

• Freeze – Perfect for berries and beans. Freeze on a tray then break up and put in a plastic bag/box so they don't stick together. Blanche beans in boiling water for two minutes. Plunge in cold water then freeze in bags. Braised red cabbage freezes well. Stone plums and freeze in a sugar syrup (9 oz. sugar to 1 pint water, just heat it up until the sugar dissolves). Cook the plums in the syrup gently, then cool and freeze. Half a pint of syrup is enough for one pound of fruit. Puree strawberries and apples before freezing. Also freeze sliced apple dipped in water with lemon juice added. Clamping – storing excess root veg under straw on your plot for the winter – is another option. Also, dry herbs in warm air.

COMPANION PLANTING

Planting beneficial plants alongside or among other crops can be useful for three reasons:

• They can improve vegetable yields.

• Companion planting can improve flavour.

• You don't have to use chemicals to control pests.

Deterrents

Strong smelling plants help deter some flies. For instance, the bean aphid may avoid your bean crop if you plant the scented herb summer savory alongside. The smell of tomatoes puts off asparagus beetle. Spray garlic solution on your roses to repel aphids. Thyme does a similar job.

Sacrificial decoy plants such as nasturtium planted with brassicas such as cabbages attract caterpillars away. Nasturtiums will protect tomatoes and cucumbers against whitefly. Basil will tempt whitefly well away from tomatoes.

The smell of French marigolds repel whitefly from tomatoes and can lure aphids away from beans. Marigolds, which can take over plots if not watched, also attract beneficial insects, including ladybirds, lacewings and hoverflies, which eat aphids. However, some theories suggest an insect will simply look for the colour of the plant it wants to lay its eggs on, so confuse them by mixing up crops in small numbers rather than planting rows.

Attractants:

• Pot marigolds attract hoverflies, which lay eggs which eat aphids when they hatch.

• The smell of mint confuses pests of carrots, tomatoes, alliums and brassicas.

• Spring onions or chervil are often planted among carrots because their smell will deter carrot fly.

• If left to flower, fennel and parsnips attract hoverflies, which prey on aphids.

• The small of garlic chive also confuses carrot root fly.

• Lavender attracts pollinators and its smell can deter aphids from carrots and leeks.

• Borage among the strawberries attracts pollinators and could improve flavour.

• Wormwood can deter aphids and flea beetles from attacking neighbouring plants, while attracting hoverflies, lacewings and ladybirds, which eat aphids.

• The 'three sisters' method includes squash as a weed suppressant and living mulch, sweetcorn, and beans, which climb the corn and provide it with nitrogen.

Boosters:
• Lupins, peas and beans, and sweet peas benefit the soil by taking nitrogen from the air and storing it in their roots.

• Yarrow brings vigour in other plants and accumulates phosphorous, calcium and silica.

Flavour enhancers:
• Basil seems to improve the productivity of aubergines and peppers and improve the flavour of tomatoes and lettuce.

ORGANIC SUPPLIERS

I t was the University of Sussex's Professor Dave Goulson who found widespread evidence of neonicotinoids in plants in garden centres. This opened gardeners' eyes to the ubiquity of the bee-harming pesticides that are being widely used on plants they were buying, without them realising. This has led to more people thinking about buying organic plants if they don't want to grow their own. They are rarely available in retailers but are accessible online.

Cambridgeshire-based Delfland Nurseries grows 40m plants a year under 3ha of glass and turns over £2m. Half of production is organic. Co-owner Jill Vaughan says the organic market is 'steadily growing' each year because younger people are more interested in what's in their food and being pesticide-free are less keen on sprays and artificial fertilisers than older allotment holders, adding, 'Overall, organic growers as a total are growing in number as people drop off the other end.' She means when old gardeners die, chemical use goes down because newcomer young gardeners don't use artificial chems and ferts like their parents and grandparents often did.

Salads such as tomatoes and lettuces are top sellers at Delfland - the same as the non-organic market.

Vaughan says that sciarid fly is the biggest concern in organics because they prefer organic compost to compost with artificial fertiliser in it. She says biological controls have to be 'spot on' and uses a mix of products which it also sells to home gardeners – Swirskii predatory mites for red spider mites, Aphidius parasitic wasps for aphids, glue traps for flying insects, phytoseiulius for mites, nematodes for slugs and encarsia parasitic wasps for whitefly. She adds that watering and correct hygiene is important too.

For the home gardener, she recommends enviromesh on brassicas and carrots through the season until September to guard from cabbage root fly, carrot fly and cabbage white butterfly. Take it off in September for a month to stop whitefly building up, then cover with coarser winter netting to guard from pigeons.

Walcot Organic Nursery in Evesham, Worcestershire, says the market for organic fruit trees is growing and sells 12,500 trees a year, with cherries booming at present. Walcot's Chris Ford said people are increasingly keen on organics because they are concerned about climate change and what inputs have gone into plants. The nursery uses a five-year rotation and greasebands on trees as protection against winter

The organic market is 'steadily growing' each year because younger people are more interested in what's in their food ...

moth caterpillars and under Soil Association organic rules can use pyrethroid insecticide sprays if needed.

Walcot advises customers keep 1sqm around the base of trees clear of weeds and grass and mulched with green compost or straw.

Gwynfor Growers in Llandysul, West Wales, is not certified organic but owner Steve Hipkin operates organically, using Fertile Fibre Vegro compost. Moorgold and Melcourt Sylvamix Natural are also Soil Association organic certified.

Hipkin, who grows on one acre, says it is 'really important people realise plants sold in garden centres are laced with neonicotinoids'. He says imidacloprid is 'quite scary' and he is glad it is restricted. He uses nematodes on vine weevil, though he says some fellow green growers use Met52, which contains spores of the pathogenic fungus Metarhizium anisopliae, which are less effective at low temperatures. He uses spring and autumn nematode doses, but says in other areas just a spring dose could be enough.

Veganically-grown leek seedlings grown and sold at Hulme Community Garden Centre in Manchester.

The basics are to feed the soil, have healthy growing areas and be careful with your resources ...

Growing just dozens rather than hundreds or thousands of different plants means there are now big blocks of susceptible crops. Hipkin has a national collection of rosemary and grows perennials and fruit trees.

Chase Organic's Mike Hedges says seaweed sales are rising, particularly in animal feed. Chase uses UK seaweed from North Atlantic shores and says seaweed is a renewable resource if you leave 15cm of stalk when cutting by hand, which means it can be harvested every four years. He says getting new people into gardening is the problem, rather than getting people to go organic. 'If you are going to start gardening you are now far more likely to go straight in organically and not use glyphosate or other chemicals in your garden'. He says the number of animal-free gardeners is growing too:

'If you have a choice between a product with bits of animal in or not, people just have a better feeling about animal-free. It's not so much a vegetarian or vegan thing, it's what you are putting on your garden. A lot of people get a bit squeamish about bone on their garden and don't want to use it unless they need to. Gardening leans towards women and mums with kids don't fancy blood in the garden where the kids are going to play. We use green waste, alfalfa, seaweed and comfrey instead – it is all mineral or plant-based.'

Chase was founded in 1912 and was in a long-term joint venture with the Garden Organic charity to distribute an organic gardening catalogue, which Chase now distributes alone.

Founder Major L.H. Chase was concerned that his crops were being polluted by rising levels of dirt and soot in the air in the early twentieth century. He invented the Chase Cloche, a modular wire and glass crop protection system that kept plants clean and allowed a longer growing season and improved growth.

Chase came up with the Second World War slogan 'cloches against Hitler' then bettered it with 'Dig for Victory', which caught on. 'Chase' also sells another long-established innovation, QR herbal compost activator, developed by Soil Association pioneer Maye Bruce.

The charity Garden Organic's Sarah Brown says organic growing all depends where you are 'on the spectrum' from very deep green with no animal inputs to people who will throw anything on the garden if they think it will help plants grow. According to Brown, being organic is not just about what you put on the land, but the whole inter-dependency of all the life forms in your area. 'It's not just not using chemicals, it's about "do I need to obliterate these weeds?" Maybe I can just manage them. And with plant health and disease it's about prevention rather than cure. The organic grower feeds the soil, not the plant.'

Brown acknowledges that organic guidelines can be preachy and we can't all be 100 per cent organic, but the tone of guidelines is important so as to not put people off. The basics are to feed the soil, have healthy growing areas and be careful with your resources. Not using chemicals comes after that, which by then seems obvious. She says blood, fish and bone are 'amber', while toxic chemicals get a red light, and that cutting out animal products from gardening is a personal choice rather than something Garden Organic stipulates.

Poyntzfield Herbs in Ross & Cromarty uses a biodynamic closed system in which they produce six tonnes of its own vegetable compost on site a year to produce 400 varieties of herbs.

Duncan Ross says, 'We don't use anything at all. It's not necessary. We're non-intensive and use our own organic garden compost and have no issues with pests and diseases.' Ross does bring in some seaweed, but mostly uses composted grass cuttings and garden waste.

He says, 'It is part of the biodynamic way of thinking to try and create everything within your own garden without inputs and keep a closed circle within your farm or garden to make it self-sufficient and totally sustainable. There's no need

Veganic chard seedlings.

for animal input.' Ross says parsley, sage, rosemary, thyme and mint are top sellers, mirroring the rest of the herb market.

He says low input and low intensity growing with medium outputs is possible under the self-reliant system he uses. Ross says veganic producer Iain Tolhurst is 'the man' in his sector.

Tolhurst Organic Partnership grows vegetables on 8ha at Whitchurch-on-Thames, Oxfordshire, and has held the organic symbol for 40 years. Tolhurst was the first to attain the Stockfree Organic symbol in 2004 and has had no grazing animals and no animal inputs to any part of the farm for the last ten years. It supplies weekly veg boxes, fruit and bread to more than 200 customers around the area.

Tolhurst advocates seven-year rotation, extensive use of green manures, a closed system with no animal manure or fertiliser use, and using wild areas to attract beneficial creatures to create a balanced ecosystem that does not need artificial fertilisers and chemicals.

WILDLIFE

Peter Rabbit is one of the most famous garden inhabitants in the world. The Edwardian character created by writer and artist Beatrix Potter is an anthropomorphised animal that lives in the forests of the beautiful Lake District of England with his 'friends' and 'family'. Hollywood films, cartoons, books and other licensed products have made Peter a favourite through several generations. Peter draws millions of tourists to the English Lakes from around the world. His adventures often take place in Mr McGregor's garden. This archetypal British Victorian walled garden has rows of veg tended by grumpy gardener Mr McGregor, whose enemy is carrot-munching Peter. The rabbit escapes in the stories, although his veg theft is not endorsed by this writer.

In real life, at Hilltop, in the Lakes, do you know what happens to rabbits? I once asked a gardener, who looked after the garden at Potter's old house (she died in 1943 and left her estate to the National Trust). You guessed it. He shot them. But don't tell anyone.

This sort of story is common across many areas of horticulture, from sports grounds to parks, allotments to botanic gardens.

WILDLIFE GARDENING RULES
The first rule of wildlife gardening is do nothing. This suits a lazy gardener like me, who can't follow instructions and likes to do things his own way. My jungle allotment is great for wildlife. And it is very low maintenance. I also grow 30 different crops (albeit not very much of each).

Animals like to be left alone. When I go down the plot, the foxes slink off. The birds fly away and the invertebrates burrow. They come out, like Beatrix Potter's rabbits, when I go home. I'm not really bothered if animals do good in my garden (though many do, for instance invertebrates get rid of waste material and birds eat insects).

An untidy garden is good for wildlife. Sweeping up leaves in a wood and putting them in barrows

My jungle allotment is great for wildlife. And it is very low maintenance. I also grow 30 different crops ...

is unhelpful for the soil and wildlife because the leaves 'belong' to and feed the ecosystem where they fall.

Patron saints of healthy eating such as TV chefs Jamie Oliver and Hugh Fearnley-Whittingstall have advocated eating better, eating more naturally, and eating more veg. They've also promoted killing millions of animals. Wildlife gardening is similar. Many gardeners pay lip service to it but often don't really mean it.

CAN GARDEN WILDLIFE BE TOO COMMON?
The 'too common' syndrome dogs people's attitudes to wildlife. Examples are there are too many grey squirrels and not enough reds. Greys are non-natives. Some call it squirrel racism. There are too few sparrows and starlings now, but there used to be too many. Too many seagulls and pigeons and magpies, too few curlews and eagles.

The late animal rights campaigner Carla Lane, who wrote TV series *Bread* and *The Liver Birds*, accused park keepers of being cruel and lazy for killing Canada geese. Park keepers – who complain that Canada geese destroy grass, spread disease, scare the public and cause mess – routinely destroy their eggs and gull eggs by dipping them in paraffin or pricking them with needles.

(Letiha Pi

Wasps are a good example. People hate them and wave their arms about when they fly by. My tip is don't hate them and don't wave your arms about ...

Lane told me a few years ago: 'Park keepers are just like everybody else. They can't stand the fact that animals poo. If they put up a sign to tell the public they were doing this the majority would be horrified.' But the RSPB defended the practice: 'It is legal and entirely appropriate to moderate wildfowl populations.'

Other examples are heron and otter killing in the UK, which were once legal. Now both are illegal – herons since 1981 in the UK and otters since 1978 (1982 in Scotland). Once there were a few around again

though, it became time to change back and start hunting them again. You won't see many otters in your garden (though herons will take garden pond fish), but they are an example of what mankind can do to a native wild species. Hunting and (now banned) organochlorine sheep dip poisoning of rivers led the first English national otter survey in 1977-9 finding evidence of otters at only 6 per cent of sites examined. They are now in every county.

Bunny Guinness, a famous UK garden designer, who dispenses

earthy advice to BBC Radio 4 listeners, suggested in 2010 the best way to trap and kill moles, rats and squirrels. Guinness said:

> 'I'm intolerant of squirrels and rabbits and pigeons. I use an air rifle on them. In the country, people are more like that. I planted 1,000 trees 25 years ago, but the squirrels have come in and they are providing food for them. Coming from a farming background, I'm intolerant.'

She recommends using a Kania Trap, which crushes the neck of squirrels. Andrew Tyler, the then director of Animal Aid, said:

> 'The whole premise of gardeners killing squirrels is hateful and bigoted. It's the worst kind of intolerance. People should cherish them. But there is a concerted attempt to characterise them as vermin and a threat to the red. Gardeners who should be nurturing life and respecting life shouldn't be taking this bigoted view.'

Organic gardener Bob Flowerdew, one of *Gardener's Question Time*'s regular presenters, said:

> 'We have two million listeners and when I suggest quite rightly that rats are becoming a pest I get hate mail saying rats have a right to live. We can do without rats, mice, fleas, lice and I'd add wood pigeons to the list.
>
> 'Get real. Rats are a pest. They brought medieval Black Death. There's animal welfare and then there's common sense. I'm with Bunny Guinness. This is a serious problem. We are losing

our roots with farming and people are beginning to forget. Country gardeners still see the problem but town gardeners are not looking. The fabric of your house could be ripped to the ground, never mind your garden.'

Many now fear that the gulf between gardeners and animal lovers has stretched too far, made worse by the Government-endorsed cull of grey squirrels.

The radio gardeners' comments came after a storm about nine-month old twins who were 'mauled by a fox cub' in their east London home. Dogs sometimes bite people. Foxes are scared of people. Wasps are a good example. People hate them and wave their arms about when they fly by. My tip is don't hate them and don't wave your arms about.

HOW MUCH HAVE TIMES CHANGED?

Dr David Hessayon, whose *Expert* guides have sold 8 million copies, is a garden writing legend. Much of his advice is authoritative. But he suggests killing worms and ants. This makes the garden look better. I'm against this.

Chems and ferts maker Pan Britannica Industries, where Hessayon was chief scientist, published and distributed the books until the 2000s. PBI is now part of Bayer, the German pharmaceutical and chemical company. Bayer no longer sees Hessayon as core business, so Transworld now publishes the Hessayon guide series.

Hessayon said:

> 'Unfortunately, the range of organic sprays continues to

decline. I stick to good old Growmore and also Fish, Blood and Bone – the best of the organics. During my active years I regarded myself as a gardener who kept the environment in mind. I would use products and techniques that I felt would not harm the plants, people or the environment. There were many chemicals I would not use.'

Hessayon's books originally sprang out of his work at PBI and include numerous references to products he helped develop. The books popularised these chemical products. Dr Hessayon's advice was of its time. He gave the options available.

The stats suggest that most gardeners have a Hessayon on their bookshelves. I chose a 1986 edition of Dr Hessayon's first book, *The Garden Expert*, to compare to the *Green Garden Expert*. The 128-page 1986 guide includes 21 pages on 'troubles' and 6 pages on fertilizers.

Only a few decades ago, the chemicals Hessayon suggests include: Chlorophos and Hexyl on grubs, Slug Gard on woodlice, snails and slugs, Anti-Ant and Nippon on ants, Multiveg on flea beetles, Racumen Mouse Bait, Sprayday, Multirose, Derris, Malathion Greenfly Killer, Long-Last, Fenitrothion, Supercarb on mildew, Cheshunt compound solution on plant viruses, Crop Saver, Dithane on blight, Calomel dust on club root as well as the herbicides Alloxydim-Sodium, Aminotriazole, Atrazine, 2,4-D, Dalapon, Dicamba, Dichlobenil, Glyphosate, MCPA, Paraquat, Diquat (on weeds 'no persistence in soil-very popular'), Propachlor,

Simazine and Sodium Chlorate.

Times have changed. The EU banned paraquat in 2007 after links to Parkinson's. It is toxic to humans, as diquat can be. Malathion has been linked to cancer by Pesticides Action Network and Aminotriazole isn't used on food crops because of carcinogenic properties. Atrazine was banned by the EU in 2004 for persistence in groundwater and links to cancer. The UK ban on atrazine and simazine use in non-agricultural situations came into force on 31 August 1993. The list goes on.

Writing about fertilisers, Hessayon said in 1986 that inorganics are often extracted from the earth and 'every bit as natural as Bone Meal'. Others have 'earned the titles synthetic or artificial' but Hessayon reassures that 'plants can't tell the difference between plant foods from natural or synthetic sources' and they 'breakdown to the same nutrients' before uptake. He's the scientist and his advice was accepted and acceptable at the time.

HISTORY

The Second World War years saw radical thinking emerge in a time of crisis. This included the field of growing and eating. Rationing concentrated minds on nutrition. The restricted diet of the war years, and the philosophies of people who opposed war, had a bearing on two men who developed ideas that have grown in influence ever since.

Teacher Donald Watson founded veganism in 1944, while journalist and smallholder Lawrence Hills founded what became Garden Organic in 1954. Hills was keen to

Teacher Donald Watson founded veganism in 1944. (Janet Watson)

promote the potential of the herb comfrey as a natural fertiliser and the benefits of organic growing as a whole. He named his group the 'Henry Doubleday Research Association' after the nineteenth century Quaker smallholder who brought comfrey to Britain. Improving health and the environment has always been at the heart of both their movements.

Watson's ideas date back to Buddhism, founded in the fifth century BC. One precept is 'I undertake the precept to refrain from taking life,' which many take as meaning Buddhists should be vegetarian.

In November 1944, Watson called a meeting with five other non-dairy vegetarians to think up a title for what they were, a bit like a band thinking of a memorable name. Not snappy enough was the too-long 'non-dairy vegetarians', and the convoluted 'dairyban', 'vitan' and 'benevore'. 'Vegan' was

... once upon a time, there were no chemicals made by man used on farmland. Farmers had to work with the plants and the ecosystem to keep pests and diseases under control ...

the best they could come up with, containing the first three and last two letters of 'vegetarian' and to be mispronounced veg-an, or vegg-an, rather than vee-gan for years to come. In 1949, Leslie J. Cross defined veganism as 'the principle of the emancipation of animals from exploitation by man'.

Watson talks of the diseases that are infecting mankind from eating animal food - foot and mouth disease or BSE being one. He saw the end of animal farming as a way to:

'create a labour force big enough to do all the jobs that we so desperately need doing - coping with drought, coping with floods, coping with disease, of course. And perhaps, most critical of all, reforestation, stopping the ever-growing growth of the deserts and the ever-decreasing amount of fertile land on which Man lives and we know now that even the so-called harvest of the seas, through Man's avarice, interfering in a region where he has no business to go, has reached such a point of depletion that many species have almost become extinct.'

Lawrence Hills was a gardening writer. His ideas go back to Henry Doubleday (1810-1902), a scientist and horticulturist who imported gum arabic from acacia trees for postage stamp glue. He tried to develop comfrey to make the glue.

Hills believed in natural fertilisers such as comfrey rather than artificial ones. His ideas gained favour during the 1970s. These days, Garden Organic is seeking to increase outreach schemes for deprived areas and schools to encourage more fruit and veg growing.

The charity has five principles:
• Build and maintain soil health to support growing
• Encourage biodiversity for a resilient growing system
• Use resources responsibly with minimum damage to the planet
• Avoid using harmful chemicals to kill weeds, diseases and pests as they can damage your growing area and beyond
• Maintain a healthy growing area, rather than just pest and disease free.

Gardening old-timers who remember the pre-1939 days of kitchen walled gardens on estates say it was Growmore, the balanced NPK (nitrogen, phosphorus, potassium) fertiliser, which changed them from being organic to non-organic. Growmore is a balanced slow release fertiliser invented and produced by ICI during the 'Dig for Victory' campaign in the Second World War.

But once upon a time, there were no chemicals made by man used on farmland. Farmers had to work with the plants and the ecosystem to keep pests and diseases under control. During the Industrial Revolution, farmers started using nitrogen fertiliser. Mechanisation began, meaning farming needed less labour, while machines could apply artificial substances to help grow crops. In the next decades, scientists such as Mayer, Yvart, de Lasteyrie, Bosc and Davy studied gypsum for use as a fertiliser.

In the nineteenth century, chemist Justus von Liebig was a founding force behind the fertiliser

DNA testing has suggested that new potato varieties imported alongside Peruvian seabird guano in 1842 brought a virulent strain of potato blight that began the Irish potato famine ...

industry. Liebig identified the chemical elements of nitrogen (N), phosphorus (P), and potassium (K) as essential to plant growth. He found that plants draw carbon (C) and hydrogen (H) from the atmosphere and from water. Liebig believed that nitrogen could be supplied in the form of ammonia and recognized the possibility of substituting chemical fertilisers for natural ones such as manure. He was also influential in the creation of Oxo and Marmite.

Back then, high NPK bat and bird guano trade was a great Victorian industry, which ultimately caused environmental chaos. DNA testing has suggested that new potato varieties imported alongside Peruvian seabird guano in 1842 brought a virulent strain of potato blight that began the Irish potato famine.

Liebig pioneered experiments to develop artificial fertilisers and English entrepreneur Sir John

In gardening, the era of country house and kitchen gardens was dying as society changed and workers had gone to war ...

Bennet Lawes extended that work in 1842 when he patented a manure formed by treating phosphates with sulphuric acid, becoming the first to create the artificial manure industry. Understanding of nitrogen's role in plant growing developed and the synthetic fertiliser industry was born.

Fisons created fertilisers from bonemeal and superphosphate. ICI developed a concentrated complete fertiliser based on ammonium phosphate in 1931. Fisons and ICI agrochemicals are part of today's Yara International and AstraZeneca multinationals.

An alternative movement developed, partly in reaction to how growing plants was becoming a less natural process. British botanist Sir Albert Howard was the first to document traditional farming practices in India as an antidote to changing ways of farming. German Rudolf Steiner's organic farm emphasised the connection between the farmer, the plants, the land and the organisms that live on it. Lord Northbourne coined the term 'organic farming,' which was used in his 1940 wartime book *Look to the Land* that talked about the farm as an organism.

As worldwide strife led people to think more radically, scientists also developed artificial chemicals to help farmers. In gardening, the era of country house and kitchen gardens was dying as society changed and workers had gone to war. This was when the estate gardeners that were left had to turn to less labour-intensive ways of fertilising land, controlling pests and growing plants.

There were consequences to the rush towards chemical use. DDT was banned in the US after Rachel Carson's *Silent Spring* (1962) showed that the chemical was killing birds. This was the start of a long line of banned chemicals. Pesticides neonicotinoids and herbicide glyphosate are the latest to have been shown by some studies to harm bees and cause cancer, respectively.

In the 1950s, American J.I. Rodale's *Organic Gardening* magazine brought organic farming methods to the public. More radical ideas have followed, including the Vegan Organic Network, devoted to stock-free gardening and farming, and founded in 1996.

Who would have thought the founder of a radical worldwide movement that now numbers hundreds of thousands of followers would be a quiet, unassuming woodwork teacher from Keswick, Cumbria? Donald Watson, who lived at Chestnut Hill in the Lake District town for more than 50 years, where he taught at Lairthwaite School, was an internationally-acclaimed dietary revolutionary, coining the term 'vegan' in 1944. Watson died aged 95 on 16 November 2005.

His daughter, Janet Watson, still lives at Keswick's Chestnut Hill. Explaining Watson's revelation, she said:

'Working on his uncle's farm he had come to question what was going on and then shortly after his brother and sister also became vegetarians. His parents he always said were greatly philosophical and didn't put any pressure on their children to conform. They puzzled about it but accepted it

and let him find his own path in life.'

Watson never forgot the screams of a pig being slaughtered. He later called the farm 'Death Row for animals'.

The son of a headmaster in the mining community of Mexborough, South Yorkshire, he was born into an environment in which vegetarianism, let alone veganism, was unknown. Watson became a vegetarian aged 14, completely of his own accord. Later, this developed into veganism. He was a lifelong teetotaller and non-smoker who tried to avoid contact with any foods or substances which he regarded as 'toxins'.

Aged 15, he left school to learn joinery as an apprentice, later becoming a teacher in Leicester then in Keswick, where his hobbies were fell-walking and organic vegetable gardening. Janet Watson was brought up as a vegetarian rather than a vegan by Donald and his wife Dorothy and remains a vegetarian. She told me:

'I was very small when my parents and I came to Keswick in 1951 from Leicestershire. One of my father's main priorities was to find a house with enough land to have an organic vegetable garden. In Leicestershire he had an allotment and had to trek across the city. His dream when he came to Keswick was to have his garden outside his front door.

'They bought this house (Sandburne) with quite a lot of land, including next door's, so he sold part of the house because he just wanted the garden more than the house.

'This patch has been an organic vegetable garden since 1952. It's ¾ acre up to the road and down to the field.

'He was mainly interested in vegetables rather than flowers. His main passion was vegetables and he tried virtually everything. He had a philosophy that he wanted to grow things that were happy growing here. For instance, he tried carrots but they didn't work because it wasn't sandy enough so he concentrated predominantly on potatoes, tomatoes and all sorts of beans. He had fruit bushes – raspberries and blackcurrants - things like that.

'Because things grew well here he never put anything commercial on the soil, not even commercial organic products. He introduced a compost system early on and it now has five compost bins. He had a rotational system with that and ploughed all that back into the garden. He had a big leaf hopper, which he filled when he went out and collected dead leaves from Great Wood in Borrowdale.'

So what did he eat?

'He ate just vegetables really. Anything made from the things that he grew so well. We did feel very it was noticeable the difference in the produce straight from the ground that we ate straight away. It tastes so good when you get vegetables properly grown and you don't need to add exotic sauces.

'We had a big freezer. It didn't work well for peas and beans – it worked well for soft fruit. We made a lot of jam from soft fruits so we were self-sufficient. Bottled tomatoes lasted us through the winter. And we had very nice tomato soup. There were a few [vegetarian] cookbooks, but nothing like the market we have now.'

So, how did people react to her father's unusual way of life?

'I think there was acceptance and respect and there was puzzlement. I think people found it hard to understand. I think people still find it hard to understand. What do you have for Christmas dinner, they'd ask. I found that tedious at school.'

Janet says that Donald read Victorian evolutionist Thomas Huxley at 14. At 18, on holiday in Scarborough, he found a copy of *Vegetarian* magazine which:

'came as a great revelation to him because he realised there were other people like him in the world. He's never heard of anyone – he had no support system. Later he was very supportive of anyone ploughing their own furrow in life.

'He had great respect for his parents though they were completely orthodox. His father had mutton. Don's brother and sister became vegetarian aged 14. He didn't know any other vegetarians at the time. He'd never met others and was not inspired by anybody. It does seem like a lot of his philosophy came from within. He never mentioned he was influenced by anything he read. It all came from within. In his eyes he gave almost same status to animals as humans.'

Donald founded the vegan society in

1944 during the war, when he was a conscientious objector. He had huge classes to teach and minimal rations, though vegetarians were given extra rations of cheese. As a vegan that was not of interest to him.

He wrote and duplicated the newsletter himself on an ancient machine and sent it out to anyone interested, responding to the increasing volume of correspondence single-handed for two years. From these early beginnings the worldwide movement which exists today developed, with the word 'vegan' appearing with increasing frequency on food labelling and restaurant menus.

After retirement aged 63, Donald led fell walks in the Lakes. Later, his family joined for Donald's birthday walks. They started at Scafell Pike when he was 84 and the last one was up Latrigg when he was 94.

Janet concludes:

'He'd talk about it if anybody asked. But a lot of people didn't know anything about it. They just knew him as Don the woodwork teacher.'

The Vegan Organic Network was founded in 1996 by activists David and Jane Graham and David Stringer. Their premise is:

'Vegan-organics is any system of cultivation that avoids artificial chemicals and sprays, livestock manures and animal remains from slaughter houses. Alternatively, fertility is maintained by vegetable compost, green manures, crop rotation, mulches, and any other method that is sustainable, ecologically viable and not dependent upon animal exploitation. This will ensure long term fertility, and wholesome food for this and future generations.'

The aim is to change the structure of how food is produced.

Graham was influenced by Kathleen Jannaway (1915-2003) of the Movement for Compassionate Living (MCL). Jannaway was UK Vegan Society secretary until 1983, and then in 1985 founded MCL with her husband Jack, promoting 'a way of life that is free of the exploitation and slaughter of sentient beings that is possible for all the world's people and that is sustainable within the resources of the planet'.

David Graham says:

'Since the Corbyn phenomenon, young people it appears who voted for him have shown a powerful philosophical outlook. Facebook and social media so-called followers have gone from a few hundred to 10,000. There's an environmental interest no doubt, and it's also true there's increasing interest now about the connection between eating vegan food and how that food is grown. There's still a big understanding gap between that, which is our main challenge now on the farming and gardening side.

'We started VON in 1996 and before that we were very active in the peace movement and anti-nuclear. We recognised the climate change issue was subsuming the whole anti-nuclear thing into a much broader issue with being vegan for donkey's years.

'Some of us had a background in farming, certainly with chemicals being a major contributor to global warming, so we started VON. It's a step beyond organics and the Soil Association, not that I'd criticise that.

'We are interested in ethics and animal cruelty, so that is why we promote Vegan Organic farming. And I do it for personal reasons... [and] a mixture of ideological reasons. That's where we're coming from. Ethical reasons based on pragmatics, growing food without adding methane and nitrates to the atmosphere.'

Graham was seven at the beginning of the Second World War in 1939 and was evacuated from London to a farm in Cambridgeshire. It was a mixed farm, with animals, fruit and horticulture. He later studied at the Writtle Institute of Agriculture, then obtained a degree in social science at Manchester University where he taught.

David Graham spent a year in prison as a conscientious objector in 1955 (when conscription was still in force), when he became a vegetarian. He then hitch-hiked to India and worked with Vinoba Bhave's Land Reform movement, and with the Gandhian movement. Jane Graham was imprisoned following her occupation of the American Embassy in protest at the war in Vietnam.

The Grahams became vegan about 30 years ago because of the ethical inconsistency of vegetarianism with its dependence on animal by-products. Vegetarians are, hopefully, taking a first step. Veganism is part of a holistic outlook which embraces ecology, non-violence, and respect for all beings.

David Graham sees veganism

'only a part of a holistic outlook which embraces ecology, non-violence, and respect for all beings'. This continues from demonstrating against nuclear weapons, and war, and the continuing cultural, political and economic exploitation of people worldwide. 'We formed VON because of the growing awareness that these issues were, to a great extent, being subsumed by the ecological movement.' He says consumerism is destroying the planet.

Graham suggests that many vegans appear not to understand that the food they consume is grown using slaughterhouse by-products such as fish, blood, bone, plus animal manure, and that vegans need to make this connection.

VON published Stockfree Organic Standards in 2000 – a guarantee that food is produced according to vegan principles.

ARE THERE BAD AND GOOD ANIMALS?

People like furry and feathery stuff, not insecty stuff. But there are distinctions within those areas. Rabbits are bad and hares are good. Badgers are a bit bad, snakes are dangerous and bats are scary.

The lexicon of the gardener is of bugs, pests, invaders. The gardeners' psyche is to control the plot and control nature, just as farmers control every aspect of the land to produce food and keep down wildlife and weeds that threaten production. I'd say, make your garden the opposite to farmland – hedges, long grass, wild areas, diversity, trees, chemical-free, cover

cropped, no dig, organic matter, left alone, forest canopies, with hiding and nesting places.

Be watchful of using beneficial animals in the garden. They are caged, in unnatural environments and often mistreated, albeit inadvertently. Bees, chickens, fish and wormeries come under this category.

On the other hand, bringing back wolves, beavers, lynx, bear and seeing animals such as pine martens prosper helps re-wild the environment and create more natural ecosystems from the top (bears – I know they are a bit 'risky') to worms, millipedes, woodlice, springtails, and micro-organisms. There's an iceberg effect with 4/5 of activity underground.

Gardens are good for us. This is called biophilia. We are naturally scared of animals (snakes, wasps, bears) but still love nature. A study of 263 people in Milton Keynes, Luton and Bedford by Exeter

and Brisbane universities and the British Trust for Ornithology found residents reported lower levels of depression, anxiety and stress in areas of higher vegetation cover. But lots of studies show 'screen time' is 'disconnecting' children from nature and outdoors, meaning the future appreciation and understanding of nature and gardens is in jeopardy.

So, are some animals and birds more desirable in urban areas than others? Here's an example. The Royal Parks in London, which include Hyde and Regent's Park as well as Richmond and Bushy parks, culled more than 10,000 animals including 2,657 rabbits and 1,221 crows between 2013-17. More than 8,400 mammals and 3,240 birds were culled, including 1,734 deer, 330 foxes, 268 geese and more than 1,000 pigeons. Charity Animal Aid urged rangers to use alternatives to shooting such as removing food sources. The parks are artificial environments with limited space,

a lack of predators, plenty of food (often left by humans) and good breeding conditions. The Royal Parks insists culling is the best way to manage populations of problem species.

HOW WILD ARE GARDENS?

In the UK, 83 per cent of people live in urban areas. One in four (4.5m) front gardens are paved over. Gardens occupy a quarter of urban areas, making up half of their green spaces. But in London, there has been a 26 per cent increase in hard surfaces in nine years.

There are 29m trees in UK gardens, a quarter of those found outside woodlands. The Jennifer Owen Leicester 190sqm back garden study of 1971-2001 found 2,673 plant and animal species (474 were plants), 9 per cent of all the species known to live in the UK. At the Natural History Museum in London, in 20 years, 3,000 species have appeared in a 1.8ha area. In Belfast, Cardiff, Edinburgh and Leicester a study of 267 gardens found 1,056 plant species. The Biodiversity in Urban Gardens (BUGS) projects which ran in Sheffield from 2002-07 found, among many other interesting pieces of information, 159 different plant species on the lawns of 52 Sheffield homes. This shows how diverse gardens are.

Half of British households feed birds, there are 4.7m bird boxes and 2.5-3.5m ponds. Forget the birds. Ponds are useful though. There are six times more ponds in towns than countryside. I also advocate using animal houses in the garden. You can create 'natural' habitats too by making log piles, stone piles, compost heaps, leaf piles, bogs, long grass and weedy wild areas, as well as planting shrubs, trees and flowers, including climbers up walls. Boxes for bats, birds and hedgehogs may work. Bat boxes do best mounted on poles and facing south. They need to be made of rough wood to cling to and need a space in a box with several chambers. Bird boxes can attract cats. Spiky and noisy deterrents and being high up helps keep them safe.

Birds and insects may nest in walls, eaves and hedges, while the inside and underneath of sheds shelter many mammals and insects. Eschew feeders and bird baths, which may attract animals you might not want in the garden, and which could kill the birds that you bring in. And the food you provide might not do as much good as you think. £299m is spent on feeding and feeders for 30m birds annually. Artificially fed birds might not sing as much, and not attract mates, some research suggests. Feeding them bread or dog food might do them more harm than good. A lack of hygiene around bird feeders can lead

A wild garden area, good for wildlife, birds and insects.

to diseases such as trichomonosis (trike), salmonella, aspergillosis and avian pox spreading. Salmonella can spread food poisoning to humans.

So, best of all, is to create habitats and grow food for birds and animals to eat, while covering or deterring creatures from crops you want to keep for yourself.

IS IT GOOD TO TIDY THE GARDEN?

A 2016 National Trust TV advert, as the first step in a long-term brand marketing strategy, portrayed scenes of National Trust staff at work, including one of staff tidying leaves in a beech woodland and putting sticks from the woodland floor into wheelbarrows. The advert goes on to show a child with a stag beetle, which lives among the leaves and debris on the woodland floor. This shows the disconnect between two opposites, a superficial idea of what conservation is – working on the natural environment – and what is generally better for natural environments, which is leaving them alone.

Charity Buglife says it is never good to clear up the woodland floor. A wheelbarrow full of deadwood from the woodland floor takes away the habitat of the stag beetle, for instance. What is beneficial is that materials are gathered to make a large deadwood pile and leaf mound elsewhere in the wood, which could benefit biodiversity, but Buglife says it is never good to clear up the woodland floor.

Leading environmentalist author Chris Baines says the image of raking leaves in woodland is a very strange one to choose:

'Decay is a key part of the woodland ecosystem. Fallen leaves and wood are far better left in situ and allowed to decompose. The fungi and invertebrates that process the leaf litter form a vital vase for the woodland food web, with many creatures, including song birds, hedgehogs, shrews and toads depending on them.

'Raking up leaves in gardens is wholly acceptable, so long as the leaves are then used to create hibernation heaps in quiet corners, or to mulch planted areas.'

Raking leaves in wooded areas to clear paths and create play areas could be a good idea, however. And raking up diseased leaves, such as those damaged by leaf miner, helps stop the spread of damaging insects. All these lessons translate to the urban garden.

WHAT ARE THE BENEFITS OF SUPER ORGANIC WILD GARDENING?

Gardens serve many purposes. They can be cultivated for flowers or food, used as spaces for exercise, relaxation, solace and recovery. They can be used as places to play, meet, volunteer, and they can be part of a wider environmental aim of the owner. The role of gardening interventions in the NHS and health and care system are increasingly being cited in campaigns to promote greenspace and horticulture. But there are moral dilemmas around gardening. The good it does physically can be offset by the bad back digging causes. Taming a plot scares off wildlife.

The holistic value of horticulture is to help alleviate the effects of climate change and to help people engage with the natural world. Embracing nature and wildlife for the feel-good factor makes sense, but do gardeners really do this, and if they knew why doing this makes them feel better, would they do it more? And would reluctant gardeners garden more if they knew exactly what good it was doing them?

Large parts of modern society are increasingly disengaged from the natural world, through urban living and being immersed in new technologies. This has a number of downsides, both for other species but also for ourselves. A lack of engagement or understanding of nature and our own basic ecological needs has been coined 'nature deficit disorder'. Indeed, some now argue there is a significant rift between our modern society and our basic ecological and physiological requirements. Urban horticulture has a big role in helping city dwellers get back in touch with nature and natural processes. Horticulturists are well placed to understand the important details of green landscapes and can get the best 'services' out of these places.

Symptoms of the disorder can include reduced physical activity and related health issues based around a sedentary lifestyle; a reduction in well-being and increase in mental health problems; fewer social skills; reduced attention span/ poorer academic performance; a lack of understanding/appreciation of our own basic environmental requirements (natural cycles, where fresh water/food comes from); apathy and an inability to deal with environmental challenges such as climate change; less understanding of or empathy for other species;

and a lack of understanding of the value that natural areas and green spaces can provide. In an urban context, this includes combating urban heat islands, improving water quality, reducing the risk of flooding, providing habitat for wildlife, opportunities for recreation and leisure and also directly providing economic gains.

Plants will also be used more to alleviate the effects of climate change such as the urban heat island effect and also to insulate houses. With the climate becoming more volatile – warmer (1-4°C warmer by 2050, with 5-30 per cent more rain in winter and 20-40 per cent less in summer, less snow and frost but more drought and flood and a longer growing season), gardening and trees and plants will become more meaningful because they can absorb carbon dioxide from the atmosphere through photosynthesis and store it in the form of wood, thus reducing the impact of global warming.

A generation on from Chris Baines' seminal *How to Make a Wildlife Garden* (1986) book, gardeners are still presented with moral dilemmas about how to deal with creatures in their gardens. While most gardeners say they love wildlife, few accept most creatures onto their plots. Gardeners can learn to embrace wildlife without worrying that their gardens will suffer. Each answer offers solutions on how to bring wildlife in, safely and successfully, for the benefit of nature, you and your family and the environment.

Accepting wildlife into your space is safer, cleaner, simpler and less dangerous than you think. Of course, everyone knows it is green to

hug a slug or love a dove, but that's easier said than done. Wildlife in the garden helps control pests and diseases. You can also do your bit to try and counter habitat destruction, albeit on a micro scale.

Berry bushes and nectar and pollen providers are best for bees and butterflies. A pond will attract insects, amphibians and other creatures. Grow a wildflower meadow for butterflies and moths. Choose native species for wildlife plantings, though there are many non-natives such as buddleia and cotoneasters that would also be very useful.

HABITAT SURVEY

First of all, map your space using an old A-Z guide or Ordnance Survey map to identify what you have on your plot. Play I-spy to make finding creatures fun. Mark the old map or guide up with red dots or other colour-coded stickers to show what you have found and where. Look in gaps, corridors, streams and verges and roads and discover pockets people have not seen before.

As part of a group, you can gain evidence – a picture of local wildlife – and you will see what wildlife is around that you can attract to your garden and what they like. Using evidence you have found, campaign for improvements to help bring in more wildlife. This could be installation of bird boxes, for the council to stop mowing verges or you could campaign against tree loss by checking council planning data on the internet or by looking in the media. Going further, your group could buy threatened land, or you could simply volunteer to help other local groups or campaigns.

ANIMALS AND GARDENS

Animal Aid has long been concerned about the growing tendency to scapegoat various animal species for the vices of human beings. Some species are being targeted because they are deemed to interfere with agricultural or 'game' bird production systems; others, because they are regarded as urban 'pests' or 'aliens'.

Wild animals are already facing immense challenges from climate change, habitat destruction, pesticide use, loss of hedgerows, the urbanisation of gardens, roads traversing their environments and the ever-increasing urban sprawl. And those who do survive are often blamed for encroaching on our space. From the politically motivated badger cull to the 'gene cleansing' ruddy duck cull, wild animals pay the price for human demands.

Sometimes, the question arises of what harm growing plants does to animals. Land clearance, pesticides and harvesting machines all kill animals. To answer that, you could point out that most crops are fed to animals. Chickens and pigs convert grain into meat at rates of two or three to one one (i.e. three kg of grain produces one kg chicken meat). The ratio for lamb is between four and over six to one and that for beef starts at five to one and goes as high as twenty to one.

Buying organic helps. As does growing your own. Fewer invertebrates die in these types of food production. These systems also have more wild areas for animals to live in.

SLUGS AND SNAILS

Garden (small/black/pale side stripe), field (small/grey/flecked) and keel slugs (orange stripe) are common. There might be 200 per cubic metre buried in the soil. I'd advocate you metaphorically 'hug a slug', a bit like you might hug a tree. Gardeners drown them in beer, slice them with scissors, or give them a lingering salty death. The slug has a moist skin, so when you sprinkle salt on to it a strong brine quickly forms. The process of osmosis then begins, by which water is drawn from a weak solution (in this case the body fluid of the slug) into a stronger one. Result; the slug dies a lingering death by dehydration. Oats swell them up until they

explode. Or gardeners chuck them over the fence. They come back unless you can really hurl. Moving slugs (and many other creatures) is like mopping up water with the tap running. Many slug pellets contain metaldehyde which can kill dogs and get into water courses where it is toxic to fish. Organic slug pellets kill slugs. Hopefully, you think killing stuff is bad if you have got this far through this book.

Nematodes eat slug eggs. But the chances are you will kill your nematodes before you kill your slugs.

To deter slugs, you can take away the dark, damp places where they hide. But they mostly live underground. You might like to install electric fences at various heights for slugs, rabbits and deer. Copper, coffee grounds, wool, grit and broken glass are barriers that might put off slugs. A Cumbrian company called Grazers makes solutions that deter a range of animals, including slugs. Slugs really like vegetables, but I don't advocate growing no veg. I do think creating an ecosystem where there are predators such as birds that will control slugs is the best idea.

APHIDS

Greenfly and whitefly eat plants, especially shoots. Birds eat greenfly, so make your garden bird-friendly, but not by having bird feeders. Ladybirds, lacewings and parasitic wasps eat aphids, so creating a food chain is a good way to keep pests under control. As well as aphids, bluebottles, horseflies, mosquitoes, green capsid bugs, midges, capsids, gnats, crane flies and black rats

are unlovable but have a role in the environment, otherwise they wouldn't exist.

Washing plants in soapy water or alcohol solution kills the aphids. But you can't dip plants in a bucket so it's an inexact way of tackling greenfly. Companion planting of lavender might put them off, as might horticultural fleece or mesh. Aphids are repelled by catnip and attracted to mustard and nasturtium. Garlic and chives repel aphids when planted near lettuce, peas or rose bushes. Try spraying cold water on the leaves. Dusting plants with flour constipates them. Organic controls that kill greenfly include pyrethrum spray, or homemade garlic or tomato-leaf sprays.

Then there's red spider mite, beetles, mealy bugs and scale insects, codling moths and mullein moths. Net crops to dodge flea beetle and carrot fly. Sow seeds sparsely to restrict egg-laying opportunities. Lots of beetles are seen even by conventional gardeners as 'good'. Insecticides will

kill these – as well as bees

For mealy bugs and scale insects, diatomaceous earth powder dehydrates and lacerates them to pieces. It also works on slugs. Gardeners sometimes use methylated spirits to kill scale insects. Alternatively, prune out areas the sap-suckers are eating. Ladybirds and lacewings will eat them, as will the predator Cryptolaemus montrouzieri. Soap and neem oil will also kill them.

Codling moth caterpillars drill into apples. Pheromone traps lure in males to their deaths by smelling like females. Nematodes are an option. Or nuke them with insecticides. Or just sacrifice some maggoty apples.

Red spider mite has a natural predator, phytoseiulus persimilis. Or keep your greenhouse clean and plants well-spaced.

Birds like eating mullein moth caterpillars, which can be picked off hosts such as buddleia.

There is no reason to kill ants or worms.

VINE WEEVILS

Evil weevils are now considered to be the most serious pest of ornamental plant production. Gardeners hate them as much as slugs, snails, squirrels, etc, etc. The black vine weevil and other closely related weevil adults feed on susceptible plant foliage leaving notched edges, while it's the larvae feeding extensively on plant roots that do the most damage. Vine weevil grubs are responsible for killing plants such as potted heucheras, primroses and soft fruit bushes. It is estimated that vine weevil damage causes £30m in annual losses for growers and that total is expected to increase with the restriction of potentially bee-harming, neonicotinoid-based, pesticide control options. Overly moist compost in plant pots is their ideal home, where they can secretly eat the roots of the plants.

Nematodes eat leatherjackets, chafer grubs and vine weevils.

Controls containing the neonicotinoid thiacloprid, have been withdrawn from sale, as have other products that contain thiacloprid. As non-flying insects, weevils travel from plant to plant by walking. It stands to reason then, that a sticky barrier can stop them moving around. If you grow your own plants within a closed ecosystem, then vine weevils should not come into your plot.

MOLES

These small subterranean mammals' short, powerful forelimbs with large paws are adapted for digging. The conventional view on moles

in gardens is they disfigure lawns and meadows by making molehills. Advice from Dr Hessayon suggests that because the blind, velvet-furred burrowers bring up sticky soil that wrecks the sward, they need to be got rid of. They can cause subsidence. Their molehills are bad for mowers and for plant roots.

There are an estimated 31m adult moles in Britain – more than the number of badgers, rats, foxes and squirrels (grey and red). It's just you don't see them. They live underground. Their tunnels trap worms and insect larvae for moles to eat. Considering there is half a mole for every man, woman and child in Britain, it's surprising they don't cause more damage. Or that no-one I know has ever seen one.

Mole repellent methods are many and various but all involve elements of animal cruelty. Battery-powered mole deterrents are available that scare moles away from an area of 1000sqm. Mole catchers are an endangered species. One control is to blow moles up. Calcium carbide poison sorts them out. As does strychnine. Rather than causing a Agatha Christie-style whodunit death as many would imagine, strychnine actually, when inhaled, swallowed, or absorbed through the eyes or mouth, causes poisoning, which results in gruesome muscular convulsions and eventually death through asphyxia.

Phostoxin or Talunex tablets containing aluminium phosphide, inserted into tunnels, where they turn into phosphine gas, kills them. Farmers used to skin them and hang their pelts on fences. Moles are virtually blind so they presumably didn't get warned off. Some gardeners bury a piece of rotten meat in mole runs, others put berberis and rose prunings down there. Some bury rags soaked

in Jeyes Fluid and creosote. Others use sulphur mole smokes. Some people shoot at them when they see molehills move. Weasel droppings are meant to deter moles. Toy windmills placed on molehills are meant to annoy moles. Euphorbia latifolia (caper spurge) plant scent deters moles, supposedly. Another plant that may encourage moles to move on is the castor bean plant, since commercial mole repellents are made from castor oil. Both plants are poisonous, though. Another option is to kill mole food – worms. This also stops their casts appearing on the lawn. Chemicals such as carbendazim and chlordane are now banned. But you can use acidifiers and other products to make the area near the surface of the grass less palatable for them to live in. Or apply mustard solution to bring worms to the surface so you can pick them off. Stop using organic fertilisers or composts, which only encourage worms. Obviously, I'd encourage doing the opposite to all these methods.

Moles have territories of 2,000-7,000sqm. If a mole is killed, then another mole will take on its territory within hours.

Moles are inedible.

To repel moles:
Simply remove the soil that forms the molehill, use it for your potted plants, and flatten the area with a roller. Or let your grass grow so you can't see the molehill. Liquid mole repellents to spread in tunnels are available commercially. The smell drives them away. Ultrasound devices may work, as may prickly holly leaves placed in tunnels.

SQUIRRELS

Wildlife lovers have a particular hatred for squirrels; grey ones anyway. They are originally from North America and were released in the UK by nineteenth century landowners. They are now very common and widespread. They often visit peanut feeders in gardens. In the autumn, they spend time storing nuts to eat during the winter. They have replaced our native red squirrels over most of the UK. They eat acorns, bulbs, tree shoots, buds, fungi, nuts and roots. Occasionally, they take birds' eggs and chicks. Reds prefer smaller pine seeds so are now mostly seen in conifer forests. After years of persecution, they are now a poster conservation animal. Squirrels quickly adapt to any suitable food source available, so if you feed wild birds regularly you are likely to also attract squirrels. The answer is not to feed wild birds.

To conserve food, squirrels will sometimes stash/bury it. While this can cause damage to plants, bulbs and lawns, it should be seen as a survival tactic and not an assault on your plants. Squirrels will also eat fruit and nuts from garden trees when available. They are accused of damaging trees – this is much less of a problem than is made out. Squirrels can get into lofts and gnaw wires; block off holes in day time when they are out looking for food.

What you can do:
• Stop feeding wild birds or use 'squirrel-proof' bird feeders, balanced on greased poles three metres or more from trees.
• Add chilli powder to the bird feed.
• Potted plants can be protected from digging and burying through

the use of squirrel repellents.

• A 'Get Off'-style deterrent may deter squirrels from digging bulbs from pots.

• Or enclose them in metal net.

• Put prickly gorse or wire netting over your bulbs.

• Scarers, ribbons and balloons (preferably with eyes drawn on) can deter squirrels from trees.

• Put cones or plastic skirts around trees that squirrels may take fruit from.

• A water sprayer on a sensor works too.

RABBITS

Rabbits can cause crop loss and can look for food in gardens in the country or edge of town. Use mesh fencing of not more than 31mm and at least 19 gauge wire, at least 100cm high and with 15cm of mesh turned out at right angles at the bottom and pegged to the ground. This will stop rabbits burrowing underneath. Liquid mammal repellents can work as can dried gorse or holly sprinkled 50cm wide around vegetable beds. Rue (ruta graveolens) may deter rabbits, which avoid iris, cyclamen, foxglove, snowdrops, daffodils, scarlet pimpernel, box, rhododendron and laurel.

BIRDS

Gardeners like some birds but hate others. They like little song birds, preferably rare ones, and dislike common, larger birds that 'bully' tiny ones. Droppings are the usual complaint. Foreign invaders such as parakeets upset the existing balance,

forcing out other birds and eating their food sources, as well as possibly damaging trees. What should gardeners do about this?

PIGEONS

Pigeons thrive in our urban environment where rooftops and high buildings are like the cliff edges where they originally nested. Pigeons breed all year round and their population is dictated by the amount of food on offer. Pigeons are amiable birds, and we should all try to be more tolerant of them as they struggle to survive and feed their young. Droppings from pigeons pose no greater risk to health than those of any other garden bird. Lethal control does not keep down numbers which quickly grow to previous levels if food remains available.

What you can do:

• Stop feeding pigeons, directly or indirectly, and encourage others to

do the same. In London's Trafalgar Square, pigeons were once a tourist attraction fed by visitors. Now they are deterred with a hawk – and by a ban on feeding.

• Ensure you dispose of your litter responsibly, taking care to secure all waste food in bins with lids.

• Don't put bread and other bird feed out in your garden, as this will attract all birds, including pigeons.

• Block access to roof spaces and buildings. Netting and spikes can be humane deterrents but must be fitted by a professional humane deterrent company. Do not call standard 'pest controllers', as they will kill pigeons.

• Other pigeons will quickly re-populate the area if there continues to be an adequate food supply. Numbers will decline if the food supply is cut off.

• You can install bird control kites.

• Spikes on roosting ledges can also deter pigeons.

GULLS

Large gulls, such as Herring and Black-backed, can be causes of complaint because they mob people for food, make a noise, foul and damage roofs. They are becoming more prevalent in urban areas because of changes in their regular food supply. The decline of fishing, as well as increasing landfill, means they can come into contact with us more often, attracted by the waste food we create. Gulls are protective of their young and may swoop to ward off any perceived danger. If there is a good food supply they will nest on nearby household rooftops, as well as other buildings. Feeding flying gulls chips is a bad idea as it encourages them to bother anyone near the chip shop.

What you can do:

• Gulls are attracted by easy food, so stop feeding birds, directly or indirectly, including those in your garden.

• Take extra care with waste food as most problems with gulls are the result of people dropping fast food waste.

• Compost food at home or use the waste food recycling schemes.

• Humane deterrents, such as blocking access to regular breeding sites, balloon-kites and gull wire to prevent landing are available.

MAGPIES, JACKDAWS AND CROWS

The corvidae family are sometimes accused of killing songbirds, but they have little impact on small bird populations, or on farmed animals

where they are occasionally linked to lamb deaths. They do well in urban areas where there are lots of waste food. Nests can block chimneys and they can damage roofs. Jackdaws have white eye rings, rooks have bare faces and crows are bluey-black all over.

'Non-problem' birds

Attract tits with deciduous trees which have insects living on them. They will eat insects, berries and seeds. Blackbirds will eat worms and insects and peck at windfall fruit. Sparrows eat seeds and feed insects to their young. Thrushes eat snails, worms, insects and berries. Sparrowhawks eat other birds. Finches eat seeds. Wrens eat insects. Starlings and sparrows were once seen as problems, but numbers have dropped because of environmental factors so are now often encouraged.

There is no evidence to show that pigeons spread disease.

Stop feeding the birds and encourage others to do the same.

Take care with food storage, using airtight containers where appropriate.

Dispose of all food waste responsibly.

Don't drop litter or food.

Obstruct access to ponds with fencing and plants to deter geese.

Ground scarers, such as flapping tapes and flags can work, but should be moved occasionally as birds can get used to them.

Balloon-kites are deterrents. Scarecrows scare crows.

Deter cats with angled fence, taut wire or string fitted 10-15 cm above the fence-top, half-full plastic bottles and CDs suspended in borders (the reflected light deters cats), spiked tree collars to prevent them climbing, spiky plant clippings from thorny or spiky plants under bushes will prevent cats from using these areas to stalk birds.

Coleus canina plants, marketed under the names Pee-off and Scaredy-cat, have a smell that repels cats and some other animals from the garden.

Scent deterrents will either repel (e.g. Citronella, citrus peel) or mark a territory (e.g. Silent Roar).

Spraying cats with water to scare them is cruel.

Plant plenty of shrubs, trees, plants with seeds and fruit to attract birds.

GEESE

Geese, such as Canada, Egyptian and Greylag, are most often seen in parks and gardens, attracted to short grass and protective water such as lakes and large ponds.

What you can do

Stop feeding geese and other birds. The more food there is on offer, the more geese there will be.

Local authorities can implement other humane measures to deter geese, such as planting vegetation at the water's edge, or erecting goose-proof fencing to block access to water.

Balloon-kites can deter geese.

Should you feed birds?

If you don't like rats or squirrels, then probably not. If you can cope with these wild animals sharing the food you put out for wild birds, then yes. Birdscaping is the way to attract birds to gardens.

Moles, rats, mice, pigeons, magpies, deer and foxes – many gardeners devote a lot of time to keeping out wild animals. But there is an industry worth billions worldwide built around attracting small birds, the likes of robins, tits, finches and songbirds: in other words, photogenic birds that look cute on the bird table but won't damage the garden.

Manufacturers have made the market a year-round one by convincing gardeners that birds need food when they are nesting, as well as in winter. But do you need to buy bird food? If you do, what is the best? And are there homemade or home-grown alternatives?

The bird food market used to be simple: bags of peanuts, mixed seeds and the occasional fat ball in colder months to keep birds happy. Now it is enhanced with vitamin supplements, and seed mixes are aimed at particular birds. One brand claims to repel squirrels and rodents.

You can attract more birds without spending on shop-bought food. Make a wildlife haven with (pesticide-free) food plants, incorporate log piles, compost heaps, mown and unmown grass, fruit trees, berry-rich hedges and ponds. Finches like teasel, honesty, dandelion, lavender, evening primrose and thistles. Greater plantain, fat hen, golden rod, groundsel and cornflower will attract other small birds. Beech, hawthorn, apple (including crab), mulberry, wild cherry, common firethorn and hornbeam are the best trees for small birds. A pond provides clean water.

RATS AND MICE AND VOLES

Mice will seek access from the garden or shed to your food and home, typically through air bricks, air vents or gaps around gas, water and drain pipes, and cable holes. They can squeeze through holes as small as 25mm. Wood mice are more common than house mice in gardens. One little-known fact is that it is easy to tell if a cheese is vegan if it is labelled 'not tested on mice'.

What you can do
When you are sure the mice are not

trapped inside, block all access holes with wire wool, 'mouse mesh' or a sealant that will harden quickly.

Ultrasonic repellents can evict mice and rats. These plug-in devices emit ultrasonic and/or electromagnetic waves, which encourage the rodents to leave but cause them no harm. In the UK, 40 per cent of pest control spend is on rats and mice. This is worth £50 a year and makes up five million units.

Mice seeking shelter will also choose a location that offers a ready food supply. They also like eating soap. And cheese.

What you can do
Clean all areas where food may be present such as cupboards and floors. Store all food in cupboards that are inaccessible to mice, or in mice-proof airtight containers. Keep up this hygiene regime.

Cover over seed trays and use tree guards to protect them from gnawing.

You can bait humane traps with peanut butter or chocolate.

Release caught mice away from your home, ideally with a little food and water to encourage them to stay away. However, this may leave a nest of young without a parent, which you could take to a rescue centre, RSPCA or vet.

If you find a nest, expose it or relocate it elsewhere.

Rats like to live in burrows in gardens, often linked to pipes and sewers and close to a food supply, such as birdseed, or warm compost heaps. Black rats are very rare (1,300 in Britain) and prefer to live in roof spaces, often gaining access via climbing plants and shrubs, but will still be looking for a good food source. Cut back branches to stop them getting in. There are fewer rats in the UK than many people believe at an estimated 6.8 million, with 3 per cent living in gardens. People fear damage to cables and pipes from gnawing, as well as the deadly Weil's Disease, caught from rat urine in water or wet soil.

What you can do
Make your garden inhospitable to rats. Animal Aid says most rat infestations are the result of bird feeding. So stop feeding wild birds and do not leave waste food around in and outside the home.

Take away habitat by keeping grass short, thinning out shrubs, removing cover such as piles of wood and debris around your garden and shed, exposing their tunnels and placing obstacles in their 'runs'. This upsets them and they may relocate.

Scatter animal repellents where there are signs of rats and around sheds.

Metal cone guards around drainpipes with the wide end facing down (250mm plus) will prevent rodents climbing between the pipe and the wall. A metal mesh balloon guard at the top of the pipe will stop rats climbing up inside.

Rodents leave greasy smears where they enter and 1mm (mice) and 3mm (rats) gnawed grooves. Rat droppings are 12mm and mice 3-7mm. Rats are harder to trap humanely than mice as they avoid new things. If you catch one, take it to woodland. Go rat watching – it's the new bird watching.

FOXES

Many gardeners hate foxes. They are scared of them eating their children and pets. However, foxes are scared of people and try to avoid them. Foxes are well adapted to living in urban environments, but simple techniques designed to make your garden inhospitable to foxes can deter them. Fox numbers are self-regulating and culling does little to populations. Other foxes take their place. Hunting has little to do with controlling a pest and more to with sport. Fox problems include digging, fouling, scattering rubbish, or noise. Foxes also scream at night during the breeding season, which runs from late December to February and in October when they compete for territory.

What you can do
Ignore them.

Replace fish and bone fertilisers with plant-based ones.

Electric fences can also be helpful.

Reduce available food – make sure bin lids are secure or, if bin bags are used, only put them out just before collection.

Do not feed birds.

Don't keep chickens.

Use scents such as Scoot (aluminium ammonium sulphate), or Get Off My Garden (methyl nonyl ketone). Citronella oil may work by confusing their sense of smell. Place deterrents where you have removed faeces or on rags close to where you find an earth.

Block access points to under the shed and also in fences where you see scratches (this may deter hedgehogs which need holes under

also live in compost piles, and under sheds. They hibernate in winter so check under log piles if you are going to have a fire.

DEER

Deer-proof fences work if you are lucky enough to live near deer. Also use plastic netting and metal guards on small trees 1.2m or higher to prevent browsing. Flapping plastic ribbons, Scoot-style repellents, electric fences and water squirting devices will also repel deer and other mammals.

BATS

The flying mammals eat flies, beetles and moths. They roost in trees and built structures. Try bought or homemade bat boxes. Plant night-scented plants to attract night flying insects. Leave wild areas. Have a pond. They don't like cats or too much artificial light. Pipistrelles are most common in gardens.

fences to move from garden to garden). And place obstacles in the way of well-used trails. A vixen and cubs could also be scared off from their earths under the shed by noise from a radio.

Ultrasound deterrents are widely available.

BADGERS

Just be very happy that you have seen one. They will eat worms, and also small mammals, birds, amphibians, lizards, eggs, seeds, bulbs and wasp nests. Badgers are nocturnal and live in underground setts, usually in woodland. The UK government has introduced a cull of badgers in an attempt to stop them spreading BSE to cattle – badgers are under pressure so need all the support from ordinary gardeners that they can get. If they become a problem in the garden, try electric fencing or Scoot-style repellents on the lawn to mask the scent of worms and insects that badgers may seek – but badgers are very difficult to deter.

HEDGEHOGS

Gardeners love them – at the moment, because they are rare. They like hedges and leaf piles. Make holes in the bottom of fences to allow them into your garden. They can

CATS

Cats have a terrible reputation for killing birds, but some research say they have little impact on overall populations. However, US cats kill 1.3bn-4bn birds and 6.3bn-22.3bn mammals a year. Colourful cat bell collars warn birds. Outward leaning angled fences, spiked tree collars, scent deterrents, scented Coleus canina plants and reflectors such as CDs may put off cats.

WEASELS/STOATS

Stoats are easily recognised. They are totally different from weasels, with black tips on their tails. They are bigger – but you'd only know that if you saw them side by side, which won't happen. They eat voles, rabbits, birds and eggs and could be a welcome visitor to your garden. Pine martens and polecats are unlikely visitors.

FISH

Don't keep pet fish in ponds. Chances are you will kill them. Over-feeding them will contaminate your pond and could lead to green soup algae issues. They can't escape a badly-built pond. Sticking a shoal of koi carp in your garden pond is not creating a natural environment. Ornamental fish freed into the wild can spread parasites to coarse fish.

Fish have distinct personalities, develop relationships, talk to each other, show affection through gentle rubs, and grieve when their companions die. They can remember past social interactions with other fish and recognize individual humans. They also have complex nervous systems and exhibit pronounced reactions to contact with painful stimuli, including strong muscular contractions, rapid breathing, and avoidance.

To catch and release semi-farmed fish is cruel as hooking them and throwing them back causes them pain and stress.

Fish should be left as wild animals.

AMPHIBIANS/REPTILES

Frogs and toads like ponds (obviously) and log piles and eat insects, snails, slugs and moths. Tadpoles eat algae. Newts need stones or logs to hide under, as well as ponds to live in. Sloping sides on the pond help young amphibians get out. Slow worms eat slugs, worms and snails and will hang around your compost bin or log pile. Grass snakes might lay eggs in your compost heap. They eat...frogs. Lizards will bask

and hibernate in log piles and eat insects and plants and are found in long grass.

How to build a pond

A pond is a boon for attracting all manner of wild/freelife on your plot. Avoid overhanging trees however as they will drop leaves into the pond. Also make sure that children won't be able to play near it unattended.

Make your pond site as big as you can, and mark out, avoiding underground cables. Dig 0.75 metres deep in the centre to stop it freezing in winter. A good design is a saucer shape with gently sloping edges so animals can get in and out.

Compact the soil and remove sharp stones before placing the liner over the hole. The best liner is butyl rubber. Buy a piece sized bigger than you think you will need. Secure the liner sides with bricks when it is spread out. Place a thin layer of soil over the liner and fill with rain

A pond with sloping edges and water plants.

water, while pulling the edges of the liner so that it fits over the contours of the pond. Leave a 30cm overlap around the sides. Trim the liner, edge with turf and plant (in the spring/summer) when the soil settles a week later. Wait for amphibians, pond insects and birds to arrive.

You can also use a bought pre-formed hard pond liner, for which you will need to dig a hole. Using aquatic plants enriches the pool with oxygen, supports beneficial bacteria that eat the floaters and debris, and give frogs, dragonflies and other creatures a habitat.

Recommended water plants: water milfoil, water starwort, miniature water lily, water soldiers (floating plant). You may need to rake plants out if they take over.

BEES

Bees appreciate flowering plants. But not all of them. Neonicotinoid pesticides used to treat young plants in the nursery may be harmful to bee health, so even plants marketed as perfect for pollinators might be bad for bees. Grow your own from seed or buy from organic nurseries or the increasing number of mainstream suppliers which now sell guaranteed neonics-free plants. You may see buff-tailed, carder, red-tailed, cuckoo, leafcutter, red mason, nomada and of course honeybees (as well as wasps).

Many popular varieties of flowers have been hybridised for features that benefit gardeners, such as disease resistance, enhanced colour, flower size and bigger or longer blooms. The result of this is a reduction of nectar and pollen produced by these hybrids. So, where possible, it is best to offer native plants for bees.

Bees like the blossom of fruit trees such as apples, cherries and plums. Later in the season, brassicas such as kale and plants such as rocket that go to flower provide food. Top flowering plants for bees include: aubretia, alysum, aster, balsam, broom, buddleia, busy lizzie, candytuft, clover, coneflower, cornflower, crocus, dandelion, hebe, honeysuckle, hyacinth, hydrangea, lavender, lavatera, heather, lobelia, lupins, marjoram, michaelmas daisy, mint, oregano, phlox, poppy, primrose, scabious, sedum, snowdrop, thyme, viburnum and wallflower.

BUTTERFLIES

To attract butterflies to your garden, plant nectar-rich plants such as buddleia, lavender and honeysuckle. Let nettles and weeds grow in wild areas. In late summer, leave fallen pears, apples and plums for butterflies such as Red Admiral and Painted Lady.

For spring nectar plant: Aubretia, bluebell, clover, cuckooflower, daisy, dandelion, forget-me-not, honesty, pansy, primrose, sweet rocket and wallflower.

For late summer/autumn nectar: Buddleia, chives, French marigold, ice plant, ivy, knapweed, marjoram, Michaelmas daisy, mint, red valerian, scabious and thyme are all attractive to butterflies.

MOTHS

Moths form a large part of the diet of bats and other garden birds such as robins, great tits, wrens and blackbirds who rely heavily on caterpillars. Urban development, climate change and intensive farming have shrunk moth numbers.

The Horse Chestnut Leaf Miner kills the leaves and the Oak Processionary moth can defoliate oak trees. This species and also the Brown Tail have long hairs which are an irritant to humans.

BEETLES/LADYBIRDS

Ladybirds are regarded as beneficial to the garden as they eat lots of insects that damage plants, such as aphids, scale insects and thrips. Some ladybirds such as the sixteen-spot, twenty-two spot and orange varieties feed on mildew which also damages garden plants. There are just a couple of species – the twenty-four spot and the bryony varieties – that feed on plant material. As ever, feel fortunate if you see them, or any other creatures in the garden.

Painted Lady.

SELECT BIBLIOGRAPHY AND RESOURCES

BALICK, COX, *Plants People and Culture –Science of Ethnobotany* (Scientific American Library 1996)

BRYANT, John, *Living With Urban Wildlife* (Centaur 2002)

BURNETT, Graham, *The Vegan Book of Permaculture* (Permanent Publications 2014)

DABBERT, HARING, ZANOLI *Organic Farming Policies and Prospects* (Zed 2004)

FOER, Jonathan Safran, *Eating Animals* (Little, Brown 2009)

HALL, Jenny and TOLHURST, Ian, *Growing Green - Organic Techniques for a Sustainable Future* (VON 2006)

HESSAYON, DR D.G., *Be Your Own Gardening Expert* (PBI 1958)

KEMP, Juliet, *Permaculture in Pots* (Permanent Publications 2012)

NORRIS, Jack and MESSINA, Virginia *Vegan for Life* (Da Capo 2011)

O'BRIEN, Kenneth Dalziel, *Veganic Gardening* (Thorsons 1986)

PEARCE, Fred, *The Landgrabbers* (Eden Project 2012)

SINGER, Peter and MASON, Jim, *Eating* (Arrow Books 2006)

THOMPSON, Ken, *No Nettles Required* (Eden Project Books 2006)

WAREHAM, Anne, *Outwitting Squirrels* (Michael O'Mara 2015)

WEST, Cleve, *Our Plot* (Frances Lincoln 2011)

DVDs - Introduction to Stockfree Organics and Grow Your Own.

VON magazine Growing Green International

www.veganorganic.net
www.stockfreeorganic.net
www.gardenorganic.org.uk
www.viva.org.uk
www.vegansociety.com
www.hulmegardencentre.org.uk
www.soilassociation.org
www.animalaid.org.uk
www.wlgf.org

INDEX